MRS. MA'S FAVORITE CHINESE RECIPES

MRS. MA'S FAVORITE CHINESE RECIPES

BY NANCY CHIH MA

K

KODANSHA INTERNATIONAL LTD.
TOKYO, NEW YORK & SAN FRANCISCO

Distributors:

United States: Kodansha International/USA, Ltd.
through Harper & Row, Publishers, Inc.
10 East 53rd Street, New York 10022

Canada: Fitzhenry & Whiteside Limited
150 Lesmill Road, Don Mills, Ontario

South America: Harper & Row, International Dept.

Mexico and Central America: HARLA S.A. de C.V.
Apartado 30–546, Mexico 4, D.F.

United Kingdom: TABS
7 Maiden Lane, London WC2

Europe: Boxerbooks Inc.
Limmatstrasse 111, 8031 Zurich

Australia and New Zealand: Book Wise (Australia) Ltd.
104–8 Sussex Street, Sydney

Thailand: Central Department Store Ltd.
306 Silom Road, Bangkok

Hong Kong and Singapore: Books for Asia Ltd.
30 Tat Chee Avenue, Kowloon; 65 Crescent Road,
Singapore 15

The Far East: Japan Publications Trading Company
P.O. Box 5030, Tokyo International, Tokyo

Published by Kodansha International Ltd., 2-12-21 Otowa,
Bunkyo-ku, Tokyo 112 and Kodansha International/USA,
Ltd., 10 East 53rd Street, New York, New York 10022 and
44 Montgomery Street, San Francisco, California 94104.

LCC 68–13739
ISBN 0–87011–063–2
JBC 2077–780624–2361

First edition, 1968
Seventh printing, 1976

To my husband Paul, who always insisted on perfection

To Danny Kaye, who taught me to add love as well as soy sauce

And to my friends, who provided both healthy appetites and kind encouragement

Photographs by Yoshikatsu Saeki. The tableware and photographs appearing on the following pages have been made available through the courtesy of: Civil Air Transport Co., Ltd. pp. 13 (bottom), 67 (bottom), and 107 (bottom); Embassy of the Republic of China, pp. 13 (middle) and 107 (top); Japan Air Lines, pp. 13 (top), 87 (top), and 126 (bottom); Tōkō, porcelain, p. 98; and Yamada Heiandō, lacquer ware, pp. 77 and 126.

Table of Contents

Preface

Originally inspired by a desire to recapture the flavors of Manchurian Court food, I have studied Chinese cooking for the past sixteen years and have collected thousands of recipes. After hours of sifting and comparison, I selected a compact collection of the most delicious and exciting among these thousands of dishes—my favorite hundred and fifty recipes for this, my eighth Chinese cookbook.

I chose those recipes that I felt would provide the greatest variety of choices for every-one from the beginner to the gourmet, from the housewife searching for new, easy meals to the cook who wants exciting culinary challenges, from the shopper who wishes to travel no further than the neighborhood supermarket to the adventurer who enjoys a trip to China-town for exotic ingredients. For all these people I have designed one cookbook, because everyone is, really, a little of all these people.

The recipes in these pages have all been carefully pretested. The specified measurements and cooking times are precise to the degree that the beginner will never appear a beginner to the guests she serves. And for the cook who never quite likes to follow a recipe to the letter, I have provided general suggestions about substitutes and variations, about the nature of Chinese food and what makes a good dish. I feel certain that after trying a few recipes, you will discover why the Chinese call cooking pen tiao, "a blending of flavors," and you will find it fun and easy to give to your cooking the thought and imagination that will make it an art. Soon you will agree with people everywhere that Chinese food is one of the world's most delicious, easy-to-prepare, and economical cuisines.

Although it seems to have become customary to begin a Chinese cookbook with an old Chinese proverb, I choose, instead, to quote the most proverbial Chinese cook I know, Mr. Danny Kaye. He has often told me, and I couldn't agree more, that "money in your pocket can be stolen, but good food in your stomach—that is yours."

Tokyo
1968

Nancy Chih Ma

BASICS

GIANT WHITE RADISH

CHINESE CABBAGE

LOTUS ROOT

ARROWHEAD
BULBS

BEAN SPROUTS

GINGER ROOT

JUTS'AI

LEEK

SPRING ONION

JEW'S EAR

DRIED SCALLOPS

RED DATES

DRIED LILY BUDS

CHINESE VERMICELLI

PRESERVED DUCK EGGS

GINKGO NUTS

SWALLOW'S NEST

SHARK'S FIN

JELLYFISH

REFINED SHARK'S FIN

DRIED SHRIMP

DRIED MUSHROOMS

DRIED BÊCHE-DE-MER

COOKING STYLES

Since China is such a very large country, the term "Chinese cooking" covers a wide range of cooking methods from various parts of the land. Chinese cooking can be broadly divided into two styles: northern (Peking) style and southern (Cantonese, Shanghai, and Szechwan) style.

The emperors of the prosperous Ching dynasty were often served Peking-style dishes. Noted recipes and chefs from all of China were introduced to Peking. Great efforts were made to achieve perfection in the art of food preparation. China was blessed with abundant coal, and with the presence of a strong coal cooking fire, deep-fried and sautéed foods became an important part of Peking-style cooking.

Canton faces the South China Sea and offers numerous variations of fish and lobster recipes. Shark's fin is a special delicacy of the area. An early international port, Canton was influenced by many aspects of European culture and Cantonese dishes differ significantly from other Chinese styles of cooking because of this influence.

Shanghai cooking is noted for its many varied noodle recipes. These dishes are strongly flavored with soy sauce and sugar.

Szechwan is a hilly country where there are few marine products. As in other lands where the climate is cold and damp, methods of preserving foods, such as salting meat and fish, are highly developed. Garlic, red pepper and leek are familiar ingredients to the Szechwan cook and give a spicy warmth to the dishes of the area.

COOKING UTENSILS

In spite of the numerous varieties of Chinese food, its preparation does not require many utensils. A kitchen knife, chopping board, large pan, spatula, ladle, and cheesecloth are the essential tools. A rolling pin, a steamer with a rack, and an egg beater will also be necessary for many of the recipes in this book.

1. *Chopping board and kitchen knife (I):* The chopping board is a round section of pine. The direction of the grain of the wood keeps the knife from slipping and protects the blade against chips. The large, heavy kitchen knife is used for cutting meat, chicken with bones, and vegetables into various shapes and sizes, for shredding, slicing, dicing, chopping, and sectioning.

2. *Chopping board and kitchen knife (II):* The author designed this chopping

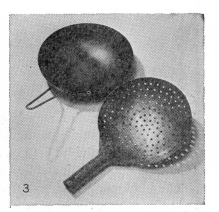

board with a semi-circular cutout that can be fitted with a container. Ingredients that have been cut on the board can quickly be swept into the container and the various ingredients for a single recipe can easily be arranged together on one plate by rotating the dish beneath the cutout on the board. The kitchen knife is narrow and has a very sharp edge. It is used for meat, fish and vegetables.

3. *Chinese pan and draining ladle:* The round-bottomed pan can be used for almost all Chinese cooking methods. The form, unlike that of a shallow, flat-bottomed pan, permits quick and easy stirring without the worry that something may fly out of the pan. Foods can be cooked quickly and evenly since the design allows a uniform heat to reach all parts of the pan. (It is suggested that with electric ranges, a crown be used to hold the pan securely.)

4. *Steamer with racks:* The steamer is made of bamboo and can be fitted with a number of racks, stacked one on top of the other, so that several different dishes can be steamed at the same time. It maintains a more constant temperature and even distribution of steam than metal steamers and thus ensures a better flavor for steamed dishes.

5. *Rinsing basket:* The basket is made of bamboo and used for rinsing and draining vegetables.

16

6. *Additional tools:* (1) metal sieve for sifting flour
(2) metal ladle that measures 1/2 cup (100 cc.)
(3) metal spatula with a long handle and a rounded edge
that is designed for stirring sautéed foods and keeping
ingredients from burning
(4) fine-meshed strainer that can also be used for sifting flour
(5) bamboo tea strainer
(6) measuring cup of 200 cc. capacity
(7) wooden spatula for mixing and sautéing rice
(8) vegetable grater
(9) bamboo whisk for cleaning pans
(10) measuring spoons and spatula for level measures
(1 T. = 15 cc., 1 t. = 5 cc.)
(11) rubber spatula
(12) bamboo chopsticks for deep frying and sautéing
(13) garlic press for both crushing and extracting juice from
garlic and ginger

INGREDIENTS

Most ingredients used in Chinese cooking are common to Western dishes as well, but there are some that are considered rare. Even these rare items can be found in Chinese food shops in any part of the world.

Giant white radish is a winter and spring vegetable that may be cooked or shredded and served raw in a salad.

Lotus root is an autumn and winter vegetable that may be braised or fried.

Chinese cabbage is frequently used in soup, sautéed, or braised. Head cabbage may be substituted.

Bean sprouts should never be overcooked. Both white and yellow sprouts are used. Fresh sprouts should be trimmed at both ends; canned sprouts should be drained before use.

Arrowhead bulb is either fried or braised. Canned arrowhead bulb is available.

Juts'ai (Allium tuberosum) is an Oriental vegetable that adds its own special flavor to spring soups and sautés. Spring onion (Welsh onion) may be substituted.

Ginger root is particularly useful for softening strong tastes and odors of fish and meat. Powdered ginger may be used but fresh ginger is preferable. The recipes in this book use slices 1″ in diameter.

Jew's ear is a kind of dried mushroom used in soups, noodle dishes, and vinegared or braised foods.

Leek is frequently used both as a vegetable and as a flavoring ingredient. Onion may be substituted.

Dried lily buds are used in soups, fried and braised foods. They should be soaked in hot water for thirty minutes and the hard parts removed before using.

Dried scallops are preserved in cans and should be exposed to the sun occasionally. Wash well, cover with hot water, and let stand two hours. The hard part should be removed before using.

Spring onion (Welsh onion) is used as a garnish and as a substitute for *juts'ai.*
Red dates are dried and used in pastries.

Transparent Chinese vermicelli is made from a kind of bean and used in soups, salads, and braised foods. It should be soaked in lukewarm or hot water to soften before using.

Preserved duck eggs are coated with a mixture of mud, lime, rice husks, wine, and spices and preserved in a dark, cool place for a hundred days. Like cheese, this food is sliced or quartered and served as an appetizer.

Ginkgo nuts are used in soups, sautés, etc. and toasted nuts are a good companion to alcoholic beverages. Both the shell and inner skin should be removed.

Jellyfish is preserved in salt and alum and should be washed in salted water and soaked in cold water. If it is thick, three to four days should be allowed for soak- ing; if thin, overnight is sufficient. Rinse, drain, and shred only the amount you plan to use immediately. Cover with hot water to curl, soak again, and drain. The remainder can be kept for two weeks if the water is changed daily.

Bird's nest is a kind of seaweed gathered by a petrel to build its nest. The best kind is as white as the petals of a water lily. Soak in water overnight, remove any feathers or dust with a pincette, rinse well, and drain in a basket lined with gauze.

Shark's fin, along with bird's nest, is considered the most delicate of Chinese cooking ingredients. It is a necessary dish for meals served an honored guest. Preparing the whole fin requires many intricate stages. Therefore, for home use, one usually buys refined shark's fin. This should be soaked overnight in hot water with a small amount of caustic soda. Cook only as much as you will use at one time and allow the rest to dry until you use it again.

Dried bêche-de-mer is used in stews. Boil it and let it stand overnight, change the water, and boil again the next day. Repeat this process for three or four days. Make a slit in the stomach and carefully remove the insides. Soak in water again for one or two days.

Dried shrimp should be washed quickly and soaked in lukewarm water before using. They may be used to make soup stock or as a companion to alcoholic beverages.

Dried mushrooms should be soaked in lukewarm water and stems removed before using. The thick, round variety is best. Fresh mushrooms may be substituted.

(not included in photograph)

Agar-agar is made from seaweed and used in jellied dishes and desserts. The white, elastic kind is preferred. Wash well, tear into small pieces, and boil in water (5 cups water to 1 agar-agar) until it melts completely. Gelatin may be substituted.

Bean curd is a white, custard-like vegetable cheese made by treating soy bean milk with coagulants, draining, and pressing. It is used largely in braised dishes.

Bean paste is made from soy beans, rice, and wheat and is used in cold noodle dishes and dressed foods.

Black peppercorn is used in preserved foods and to soften the odor of meats.

Garlic is frequently used for flavoring fish and meat, and should be crushed, chopped, or grated. In sautés, fry the garlic quickly before adding other ingredients.

Mustard is served with a small spoon. Powdered mustard is dissolved with a small amount of hot water.

Oils and fats: Animal fats turn white and their flavor changes when they become cold. You should, therefore, avoid using them for frying and sautéing. Lard is often used in pastries and chicken fat is mainly used to give an added flavor to vegetables. Vegetable oil is preferred to animal fats and wherever the recipes refer simply to "oil," the use of a vegetable oil is recommended. This would include peanut, bean, salad, and sesame oils. Sesame oil is mainly used to give an added flavor to soups and dressed foods (vinegared vegetables, bean-paste-dressed foods, etc.). If you add three or four slices of ginger and a two-inch length of leek to five cups of oil, heat, and remove the ginger and leek when browned, your oil will have a new, improved flavor and aroma. Deep-frying oil can be used again and again if it is properly stored. It must be strained through a sieve lined with cotton and kept in a covered container.

Oriental cornstarch is heavier than its Western counterpart. If Western cornstarch is used, the quantity should be slightly increased.

Oriental vinegar is not as strong as its Western counterpart. Decrease the amount slightly if you are using Western vinegar.

Oyster sauce is obtained from raw oysters and is usually canned or bottled. It is used for sautéing meats.

Red pepper is used fresh, but powdered red pepper or tabasco may be substituted.

Rice wine is made of fermented rice. The wine mentioned in the recipes refers to rice wine, but cooking wine, sherry or cognac may be substituted.

Sesame seeds are used in small amounts for dressed foods and pastries. Both black and white sesame is used and toasting enhances the flavor.

Star aniseed is shaped like an eight-pointed star and is used in braised fish, beef, and chicken dishes.

Soy sauce is made of fermented and brine-processed soy beans. *Dán jiàng you* and *nóng jiàng you* are two Chinese soy sauces. The first has a light color and a delicate taste and is used in dishes where a heavy soy flavor is undesirable. The latter is dark and thick, yet still not too strong. It contains molasses and is mostly used in restaurants. Japanese soy sauce is made with the addition of malt and is highly recommended. Western soy sauce is more concentrated and salty than any of the sauces mentioned above. If Western soy sauce is used, the quantity should be reduced considerably.

Sugar and salt for everyday use will be sufficient for most of the recipes in the book, some recipes do, however, call for crystal sugar.

Sweet bean paste is used as a pastry filling. Red beans are boiled until tender and then cooked with sugar until the consistency becomes soft and slightly tacky.

Tangerine peel is a subtle flavoring for meat and poultry dishes (especially duck) and should be soaked in lukewarm water for fifteen minutes, washed, and rinsed.

CUTTING METHODS

Cutting ingredients into various shapes and sizes does not require great skill. There are a number of traditional cutting methods that you can easily master with a little practice, or you may cut ingredients to your own liking and arrange them attractively on serving plates. What must be remembered in both cases is that each dish usually contains two or more main ingredients that must be cut in the same way. There are two reasons for this: all main ingredients must be cooked together for a given length of time, and dishes can be served more attractively when the ingredients have been cut in this way. Foods that must be cooked for a rather long time should be cut into large sizes; foods that require a short cooking time should be cut into small sizes. Meat should always be cut perpendicular to the grain.

1. *Slicing:* cut thinly; slice Chinese cabbage diagonally
2. *Shredding:* cut into fine, thread-like strips, 1″ to 2″ long; meat is cut perpendicular to the grain
3. *Chopping:* first shred and then cut shreds into small pieces
4-5. *Chopping leek:* shred the end and chop
6-8. *Chopping onion:* halve, slice with the grain, and chop
9. *Dicing:* cut into 1/4″ to 1/2″ cubes
10. *Sectioning:* cut into pieces 1″ to 2″ long
11. *Wedging:* cut into small, triangular sections

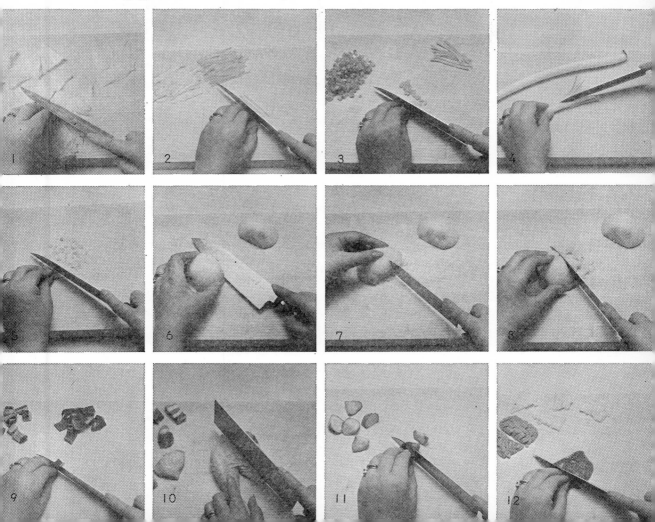

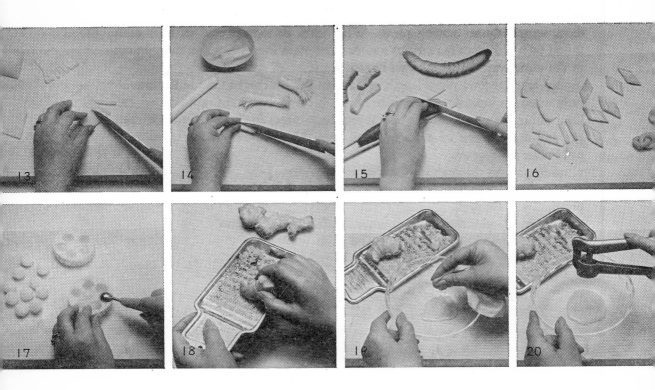

12. *Scoring:* surface-cut such foods as liver and squid in a lattice pattern; if pieces are thin, cut on a slant

13. *Fan cutting:* slice 1/8″ thick, and make cuts into half the length of the slice, leaving spaces between the cuts

14. *Flower cutting:* cut leek into 2″ lengths, shred both ends, soak in water and drain

15. *Half slicing:* use chopsticks as stops to prevent the knife from completely cutting through such foods as cucumber and abalone; cut down only as far as the chopsticks permit

16. *Half-moon cutting:* cut such vegetables as bamboo shoots and carrots into half-moon shapes; make the straight edge thinner than the curved

Stick cutting: shred thickly

Diamond cutting: cut almost any kind of vegetable into diamond shapes

Ringing cucumber: slice thinly and discard the ends; remove the centers and make a small cut in one ring so that it can be joined with another

17. *Balling:* use this scooping method for fruit and vegetables

18-20. *Juicing:* grate fresh ginger and squeeze through cheesecloth, tissue, or garlic press

COOKING METHODS
Deep frying (4 variations)

1. Fry without batter or flour coating. Use a high heat (356°F.) for foods that should be cooked rapidly; use a medium heat (338°F.) for foods that require a longer cooking time.

2. Season ingredients and coat with cornstarch. Use slightly lower heats than above.

3. Season and coat with a mixture of cornstarch and eggs or water. Wheat or rice flour may be substituted for cornstarch. Use heats from 300° to 340°F.

4. Season and dip ingredients in whipped egg white. Use clear, new oil so that foods will be a clean, white color when served. Use heats from 285° to 300°F.

Enough time must be allowed for seasoning ingredients before they are fried. Chicken, white-meat fish, shrimp, and prawn are usually seasoned with a mixture of salt and wine. Beef, pork, and liver are seasoned with soy sauce, ginger, etc. Ingredients should be marinated for ten or fifteen minutes before frying. Whole fish should always be served hot. Fry it again for a moment or reheat in the oven before serving if it has been allowed to cool. The oil should be hottest before ingredients are added since it will lose heat when ingredients are put in. When the oil begins to regain its original intensity, the fire can be adjusted to the proper temperature.

Sautéing

Foods should not be sautéed for a long time. Those that require a longer cooking time should be parboiled or deep fried quickly before sautéing. The skillet should be heated first before the oil is added, and the oil should be allowed to heat well before ingredients are added. Green vegetables will have a brighter, fresher color if a little salt is first sprinkled in the oil. It is a good idea to pre-measure seasonings and sauce ingredients so that they are ready at the moment they are needed. Start to sauté with the ingredients that require the longest cooking time and add others according to the time they will require. A special way to season a sauté is to cook such ingredients as leek, garlic, or ginger before the others. They will give the oil itself an added flavor and aroma. Also, a little sesame oil or chicken fat may be added to the pan before the food is transferred to a serving dish to give the food a richer flavor.

Braising

Vegetables, meat, fresh and dried fish may be braised in soup stock, soy sauce, salt, sugar, and wine. Ingredients are cut in large pieces and cooked over a low heat for one to two hours. Braised dishes have the attraction of retaining their flavor and allow you to cook large quantities and reheat for two or three days.

Steaming

The steamer should be well preheated and ingredients should be dried with a cloth before you begin. Use a high heat for dumplings, sponge cake, etc., and a low heat for foods that require a long cooking time. The lid must not be removed during steaming or a constant heat will not be retained. Steaming is also a good way to reheat leftovers.

CORNSTARCH SAUCES

Cornstarch in marinades tenderizes raw meat and in sauces serves another very practical purpose. The juices from cooked foods that are so necessary to the enjoyment of eating are, unfortunately, difficult to eat with chopsticks. Therefore, Chinese cooks have long thickened these juices with cornstarch so that they adhere to the food itself and can be thoroughly enjoyed. Dishes served with these sauces should not be concentrated or salty and should not be allowed to cool before the sauce is poured over them. The cornstarch should be well dissolved in water before it is added to the sauce and should be stirred well to prevent lumps and allow for a smooth sauce.

SOUP STOCKS

The following three soup stocks are repeatedly used in Chinese cooking:

1. Whole-chicken stock

1 whole soup chicken	*5 slices ginger*
1 leek, halved and browned	*30 cups water*

Place chicken, leek and ginger in water, cover and bring to a boil. Lower the heat and boil gently until half the stock has boiled away (about 1½ hours). Skim the foam from the surface of the water continually. Strain.

Note: The chicken may be used as an appetizer or in a salad. Spring chicken may be substituted for soup chicken and the cooking time reduced to only 30 minutes, but the stock will not be as rich.

2. Chicken-bone stock

the bones of one whole chicken	*4 slices ginger*
1 leek, halved and browned	*8 cups water*

Wash bones to remove smell. Place bones, leek and ginger in the water and heat to boiling. Lower heat and simmer 1 hour. Continually remove foam from surface of the stock. Strain.

3. Pork stock

1/4 lb. lean pork

2 T. oil

1 leek, shredded

4 slices ginger

6 cups water

Slice pork. Heat oil and sauté pork, leek and ginger until color of pork changes. Add water and bring to a boil. Lower heat and continue cooking 30 minutes.

DIPS

Cold dishes and deep-fried foods are usually served with a dip. In many cases soy sauce, salt, vinegar, mustard or tomato catsup are used as dips. Sometimes special dips are prepared to accompany certain dishes.

Red pepper oil should be used sparingly with steamed meat dumplings and noodles and can be simply made by adding 1/2 T. of powdered red pepper or 2 T. of fresh, shredded red pepper to 1 cup of hot sesame oil. Heat and sieve. Tabasco may be substituted for red pepper.

Salt mixture is often served with fried foods and can be either 7 parts of ground black peppercorn to 3 parts of salt, or 5 parts of each.

Vinegared soy sauce accompanies many foods well. Mix vinegar and soy sauce to taste.

In a Chinese home, it is difficult to find many condiments on the table. We believe that the food should be perfectly seasoned in the kitchen before it reaches the table and shouldn't need even one extra grain of salt. To request the salt shaker is to insult the cook.

SALAD DRESSINGS

When making a salad, you should carefully choose your ingredients and take special pains about their arrangement on the serving dish. The dressing should be blended well and poured just before eating. Any of the following dressings may be used for the salad recipes in this book. Why not try them all and remember your favorites.

1. 1 T. dry mustard, 4 T. soy sauce, 4 T. vinegar, 2 T. sesame oil and a dash of monosodium glutamate.

2. 3 T. chopped onion, 2 T. soy sauce, 4 T. vinegar, 1 t. sugar, 1/2 t. salt, 4 T. soup stock and a dash of monosodium glutamate.

3. 1 t. ginger juice, 1 T. vinegar, 2 T. soy sauce, 1/2 t. sugar and a dash of monosodium glutamate.

4.   1 t. grated garlic, 1 t. red pepper oil, 2 t. soy sauce, 1 T. vinegar, 1 T. wine, 1 t. salt, 1 t. sugar and a dash of monosodium glutamate.

5.   1 T. chopped leek, 1 t. chopped ginger, 1 t. toasted and ground peppercorn, 1/2 t. salt and 1 T. soy sauce.

6.   1 T. soy sauce, 3 T. vinegar, 2 t. sugar, 1/2 t. salt, 1 t. red pepper oil and a dash of monosodium glutamate.

7.   1 t. red pepper oil, 2 T. soy sauce, 1 T. vinegar, 1 T. sugar and 1/2 t. salt.

MEASUREMENTS AND ABBREVIATIONS

1 cup = 200 cc.
1 tablespoon = 1 T. = 15 cc.
1 teaspoon = 1 t. = 5 cc.
1 slice ginger = a slice 1 inch in diameter
1 inch = 1″
1 pound = 1 lb.
1 ounce = 1 oz.

SPRING

Whole Fried Chicken
Braised Chicken Drumsticks
Chopped Chicken with Lettuce
Bird's-Nest Balls and Braised Mushrooms
Fried Quail with Asparagus
Jellyfish and Chicken Appetizer
Fried Garnished Toast
Sautéed Prawns with Chili Peppers
Sautéed Scallops
Deep-Fried Shrimp
Shrimp Balls
Braised Bêche-de-Mer with Leek
Cold Soy-Sauce Beef
Braised Beef or Veal
Sautéed Liver and Leek
Barbecued Spareribs
Sautéed Pork with Green Peas
Egg Fu Yung
Scrambled Eggs with Spring Onion
Steamed Egg Custard
Egg Rolls
Celery and Egg Appetizer
Sautéed Vegetables with Omelet
Braised Asparagus
Stuffed Carrot Rolls
Pickled Vegetables
Braised Lima Beans
Braised Bamboo Shoots and Mushrooms
Fried Mushrooms
Fried-Fish Soup
Whole-Chicken Soup
Egg Flower Soup with Spinach

香 **Whole Fried Chicken**
酥
鷄　1 *whole spring chicken (about 2 lbs.)*
2 *T. wine*
1 *T. freshly ground black pepper*
1 *t. salt*
1/2 *t. sugar*
1 *clove garlic, chopped*
1 *leek, chopped*
1 *egg*
2 *T. flour*
deep-frying oil
parsley sprigs

Dress chicken, sprinkle with wine and let stand 5 minutes. Rub well, inside and out, with pepper, salt and sugar. Mix garlic and leek and put in cavity of chicken. Place chicken in a bowl and steam over high heat until tender (about 1 hour). Beat egg lightly and mix with flour. Brush egg-and-flour batter over chicken, heat oil to 330°F. and deep fry for 15 minutes over low heat. Use ladle to pour hot oil over chicken wherever it is not submerged in oil. To make chicken very crisp, turn heat high for a short time before removing. Garnish with parsley, cut in half, and serve hot or cold. SERVES 4

醬 **Braised Chicken Drumsticks**
油
鷄　color—page 38
腿
1 *leek or small onion*
6 *chicken drumsticks*
4 *slices ginger*
3 *T. wine*
5 *T. soy sauce*
1/2 *T. sugar*
1 *t. black peppercorns*
2 *T. sesame oil*

Cut leek into 3″ lengths (if using onion, slice). Put drumsticks in pan of water and boil 10 minutes. Discard water. Add leek, ginger, wine, soy sauce, sugar and peppercorns and simmer over low heat for 25 minutes. Add sesame oil before removing from heat. Allow chicken to soak in juices until served.

SERVES 6

29

菜包鶏鬆 Chopped Chicken with Lettuce

color—page 37

1/2 lb. chicken
1/4 lb. ham
1 head lettuce
1 egg
1/4 t. salt
5 T. oil

1 T. chopped leek
2 T. wine
1 T. soy sauce
1/2 t. tabasco or cayenne pepper
1 t. cornstarch
1 T. water

Bone and chop chicken, chop ham, and wash and drain lettuce. Beat egg with salt, heat 2 T. oil, scramble and set aside. Heat 3 T. oil and sauté chicken over high heat until color changes. Add leek, wine, soy sauce and tabasco and continue cooking until chicken is tender. Add ham and scrambled egg, mix cornstarch and water and add to thicken. Arrange on platter with lettuce and serve hot.

SERVES 4

Variation: Substitute dove or quail for chicken.
Note: Chicken mixture is rolled in individual leaves and eaten with the fingers.

蒸燕窩丸子 Bird's-Nest Balls and Braised Mushrooms

1 1/2 cup prepared (Page 19) bird's nest
3/4 lb. white-meat fish fillet
1 oz. pork fat
4-5 T. water

INGREDIENTS A:

1 egg white
2 t. wine
1 T. cornstarch
1/2 t. salt
1/2 t. sugar
1/2 t. ginger juice
dash of monosodium glutamate
10 dried mushrooms
3 T. oil
2 t. sesame oil
dash of monosodium glutamate
mustard

INGREDIENTS B:

1/2 T. sugar
2 T. soy sauce
1/2 cup soup stock

Separate prepared bird's nest into small shreds. Mince fish and pork fat, gradually adding water. Add *Ingredients A* and mix well. Form small balls with a tablespoon (Page 54) and roll in bird's-nest shreds, coating evenly. Steam over high heat for 15 minutes. Prepare mushrooms (Page 19), heat oil and sauté over high heat for 3 minutes. Add *Ingredients B*, lower heat and simmer 20 minutes. Remove from heat, sprinkle with sesame oil and monosodium glutamate, arrange with bird's-nest balls on plate and serve hot with mustard.   SERVES 4

炸 鵪 鶉 Fried Quail with Asparagus

5 *quail*
2 *T. wine*
3 *T. soy sauce*
deep-frying oil
1 *lb. fresh green asparagus*
3 *T. oil*
1 *t. salt*
1/2 *t. sugar*
1 *T. wine*

Clean quail, halve lengthwise, marinate in wine and soy sauce for 10 minutes and drain. Heat oil to 360°F. and deep fry until crisp. Remove hard end of asparagus, halve, place in boiling water with a dash of salt and simmer until tender. Heat oil and sauté asparagus over high heat until coated with oil. Add remaining ingredients, stir well, arrange with quail on serving platter and serve hot.   SERVES 5

拌 海 蜇 鷄 糸 Jellyfish and Chicken Appetizer

2 *cups shredded jellyfish (Page 18)*
1 *cup shredded boiled chicken*
2 *T. vinegar*
3 *T. soy sauce*
1 *t. mustard*
2 *T. sesame oil*

Mix prepared jellyfish and chicken. Mix remaining ingredients and pour over jellyfish-chicken mixture just before serving. Serve cold.

Sauce variation: 4 T. ground sesame seeds, 4 T. water, 1/2 t. sugar, 4 T. soy sauce, 1 T. vinegar, 3 T. sesame oil, and 2 to 3 T. red pepper oil (Page 25).

炸 魚 拖 Fried Garnished Toast

6 slices bread
1/4 lb. white-meat fish
3 T. water
1 t. wine
1/2 t. salt
1 t. oil
1/2 egg white
2 t. cornstarch
1 T. finely chopped ham
1 T. finely chopped parsley
deep-frying oil

Remove crust from bread and cut into thirds. Mince fish, gradually adding water. Mix fish with wine, salt, oil, egg white and cornstarch and divide into 18 equal portions. Spread on bread, sprinkle with ham and parsley and press lightly to make garnish adhere. Heat oil to 330°F. and gently drop bread into oil, fish-spread side down. Deep fry until bread browns slightly, and drain on absorbent paper. SERVES 6

Variation: Halve 9 walnuts and press into garnish before frying.

宮 保 明 蝦 Sautéed Prawns with Chili Peppers

6 prawns
2 leeks
8 chili peppers
1 egg white
1 T. wine
1 T. cornstarch

deep-frying oil
3 T. oil
2 slices ginger
1/2 t. grated garlic
1 T. soy sauce
1/2 T. sugar
1/2 t. salt
1 T. vinegar

Shell and devein prawns, remove tails and slit backs. Cut into three pieces and make a slit in each to prevent shrinking. Cut leeks into 2″ lengths. Halve chili peppers and remove seeds. Mix egg white with wine and cornstarch. Dip prawns in egg-white batter, heat oil to 360°F. and deep fry until slightly brown. Heat oil and sauté leek, chili pepper, ginger and garlic over high heat for 1 minute. Add remaining ingredients, bring to a boil, add fried prawns, stir and serve.

SERVES 4

炒 鮮 貝 Sautéed Scallops

8 scallops (about 3/4 lb.)
1 t. ginger juice
1 t. cornstarch
4 dried mushrooms
2 oz. snow peas
2 oz. bamboo shoots
4 T. oil
1/2 cup soup stock or water
1 T. wine
1/2 t. salt

1/2 t. sugar
1 1/2 t. cornstarch
1 T. water

Wash scallops in salted water, remove thin skins and hard parts, cut each into 5 or 6 pieces and sprinkle with ginger juice and cornstarch. Prepare (Page 19) and slice mushrooms. String snow peas, parboil in salted water and drain. Slice bamboo shoots. Heat oil and sauté scallops over high heat until color changes. Add vegetables and cook until tender. Add soup stock, wine, salt and sugar and bring to a boil. Mix cornstarch and water and add to thicken. Serve hot.

SERVES 4

炸
蝦
仁 ### Deep-Fried Shrimp

3/4 lb. shrimp
1/2 t. salt
dash of pepper
1 t. wine
1 T. cornstarch
deep-frying oil
tomato catsup or cocktail sauce

BATTER:
1/2 cup flour
1/2 t. baking powder
1/2 T. black sesame seeds
1/2 T. chopped ham
1/4 cup water

Shell and devein shrimps. Sprinkle with salt, pepper, wine and cornstarch and let stand 20 minutes. Mix batter ingredients and add shrimps. Heat oil to 335°F., drop shrimps in, one by one, and deep fry until crisp. Serve hot with tomato catsup or cocktail sauce.   SERVES 4

炸
蝦
丸
子 ### Shrimp Balls
color-page 38

1 lb. shrimp
1 egg
2 T. chopped leek
1/2 t. salt
1 t. wine
1 t. sesame oil
1 T. cornstarch
deep-frying oil
salt mixture (Page 25)

Shell and devein shrimps, remove tails and mince. Mix with egg, leek, salt, wine, sesame oil and cornstarch. Form balls with a tablespoon (Page 54). Heat oil to 360°F. and deep fry until slightly brown. Serve with salt mixture.   SERVES 4

紅
燒
海
参 ### Braised Bêche-de-Mer with Leek

1 dried bêche-de-mer
1 cup small bamboo shoots
2 leeks

34

4 T. oil
3 T. wine
4 T. soy sauce
2 T. sugar
1 cup soup stock
1 T. cornstarch
1/2 cup water

Prepare bêche-de-mer (Page 19), drain and cut in half crosswise. Cut bamboo shoots into bite-size pieces, and leeks into 1 1/2″ wedges. Heat oil and sauté leek over high heat until coated with oil. Add bamboo shoots and bêche-de-mer and sauté for a few minutes. Add wine, soy sauce, sugar and soup stock, cover and cook over medium heat for 20 minutes. Mix cornstarch and water and add to thicken, stirring constantly. Serve hot.   SERVES 4

醬
牛
肉
Cold Soy-Sauce Beef

color—page 38

2 lbs. beef fillet
1 T. salt
1/2 t. saltpeter
1 leek
5 slices ginger
2 T. sugar
2 cups soy sauce

Rub beef with mixture of salt and saltpeter and let stand 30 minutes. Wash beef well, cut into 4 pieces and bind each piece with string. Cut leek into 2″ lengths. Place beef, leek and ginger in a pot with enough water to cover. Cover and cook over high heat for 30 minutes. Add sugar and soy sauce, lower heat and simmer for 1 hour. Allow beef to soak in juices until cool. Remove, slice and serve cold.
SERVES 6

紅
燒
牛
肉
Braised Beef or Veal

1 1/2 lbs. beef or veal rump   *6 T. soy sauce*
12 white onions   *1 t. sugar*
6 slices ginger   *6 hard-boiled eggs*
2 T. wine

Bring a potful of water to a boil. Cut meat in 1 1/2″ chunks and parboil for 5 minutes. Discard water. Add onions, ginger, wine, soy sauce, sugar and enough fresh water to cover. Cover and simmer until tender (1-2 hours). Shell eggs and score so that they will absorb flavor, add to pot and continue simmering for 30 minutes. Cut eggs in halves or quarters, arrange with meat and onions on serving platter and serve hot. SERVES 6

葱
炒
牛
肝

Sautéed Liver and Leek

1/2 lb. beef liver	1 T. wine
1/2 t. ginger juice	1 T. soy sauce
1 t. cornstarch	1/2 t. sugar
2 leeks	
6 T. oil	

Slice liver into bite-size pieces, soak in water for 20 or 30 minutes to remove blood, mix with ginger juice and cornstarch and let stand 10 minutes. Cut leeks into 2″ lengths, heat 3 T. oil and sauté over high heat until tender. Remove to plate. Add 3 T. more oil to skillet and sauté liver over high heat until color changes. Add leek and remaining ingredients, mix and serve hot. SERVES 4

Sweet Rice in Bamboo Leaves is thrown into water▶ on May 5 to honor Chu Yüan, poet and statesman of the Chu dynasty (300 B.C.), who, dissatisfied with government policy, threw himself into the Mi Lo River. Boats were sent to search for his body, but it was never recovered. *Top to bottom:* Sweet Rice in Bamboo Leaves (Page 121), Fried-Fish Soup (Page 45), Egg Rolls (Page 41), Chopped Chicken with Lettuce (Page 30), and Celery and Egg Appetizer (Page 42).

烤排骨 Barbecued Spareribs

color—page 38

1 lb. spareribs	1/2 t. sugar
4 T. soy sauce	1 t. grated garlic
4 T. wine	

Separate ribs and marinate in mixture of remaining ingredients for 3-4 hours, turning occasionally. Roast on a rack over medium heat until tender (about 30 minutes). Cut into bite-size pieces before serving.   SERVES 4

Note: The meat, sliced from the bones, makes excellent sandwiches.

肉丁炒豌豆 Sautéed Pork with Green Peas

8 oz. pork	MARINADE:
2 eggs	2 t. wine
1 egg yolk	2 t. soy sauce
1 1/4 t. salt	1 egg white
1 cup green peas, canned or fresh	1 t. cornstarch
5 T. oil	

Slice pork and cut into 1/2" lengths. Marinate for 15 minutes. Beat eggs and egg yolk with 1/4 t. salt. If peas are fresh, parboil in salted water. Heat 3 T. oil, scramble egg mixture and set aside. Heat 2 T. oil and sauté pork over high heat until color changes. Add scrambled eggs, peas and 1 t. salt. Serve hot.   SERVES 4

◀March 12 is Arbor Day in China and picnic lunches accompany a gay trip to the mountainside to plant seedlings. The dishes are strongly flavored since they will be served cold. *Clockwise from the top:* Barbecued Spareribs (Page 39), Braised Chicken Drumsticks (Page 29), Cold Soy-Sauce Beef (Page 35), Shrimp Balls (Page 34), and Pickled Vegetables (Page 44).

芙蓉蟹 Egg Fu Yung

1/2 lb. canned crab meat
5 eggs
1/2 t. salt
1 t. wine
6 T. oil
1/2 cup shredded leek

1/4 cup shredded mushroom
2 t. soy sauce
1/2 cup soup stock or water
1 T. cornstarch
3 T. water

Drain crab meat, remove filaments and separate into small pieces. Beat eggs with salt and mix with crab and wine. Heat 5 T. oil and fry crab-egg mixture, turning once, to form either one large omelet or smaller omelets for individual servings. Heat 1 T. oil and sauté vegetables over high heat until coated with oil. Add soy sauce and soup stock, bring to a boil, mix cornstarch and water and add to thicken. Pour sauce over omelet and serve hot.   SERVES 4

韭菜炒蛋 Scrambled Eggs with Spring Onion

1/4 lb. spring onion (Welsh onion)
5 eggs
1 t. salt

7 T. oil
dash of monosodium glutamate

Cut onion into 2″ lengths. Beat eggs lightly with salt, heat 5 T. oil, scramble egg mixture and remove to plate. Heat 2 T. oil and sauté onion over high heat until coated with oil. Add eggs and mix. Sprinkle with monosodium glutamate and serve hot.   SERVES 2

蒸蛋羹 Steamed Egg Custard

3 eggs
1 1/2 cups soup stock or water
1/2 t. salt
3 T. oil
4 oz. ground beef or mutton
1 T. wine
1 t. soy sauce
1 t. sugar
1/2 t. red pepper or tabasco

40

Beat eggs lightly and mix with soup stock and salt. Place in deep bowl and steam over low heat until mixture sets. Heat oil and sauté ground meat until color changes. Add remaining ingredients and continue cooking 5 minutes. Pour over steamed egg and serve hot. SERVES 4

炸
蛋
卷

Egg Rolls

color—page 37

4 oz. canned crab meat
1 dried mushroom
1 leek
2 oz. bamboo shoots
2 oz. bean sprouts
4 T. oil
1/2 t. salt
1 t. soy sauce
2 T. cornstarch
2 T. water
3 eggs
1/4 t. salt
4 t. oil
1 T. flour
1 T. water
deep-frying oil

Drain crab meat, remove filaments and separate into small pieces. Prepare (Page 19) and shred mushroom. Cut leek into 2″ lengths and shred. Shred bamboo shoots, and wash and drain bean sprouts. Heat oil and sauté crab meat and vegetables over high heat until tender. Add salt and soy sauce, mix cornstarch and water and add to thicken. Set aside and cool. Beat eggs with salt, heat a 9″ skillet and coat thinly with 1 t. oil, lower heat and pour in 1/4 of egg mixture. Tip skillet to cover bottom evenly (Process Photo 1). As soon as egg sets, remove from heat and cool slightly. Using chopstick or fork, peel egg sheet from skillet and set aside (Process Photo 2). Repeat process until four sheets are prepared. Spread 1/4 of crab and vegetable mixture over egg sheet (Process Photo 3). Mix flour and water, roll egg sheet and seal with mixture (Process Photo 4). Heat oil to 330°F. and deep fry until golden brown. Cut each roll into 3 pieces and serve hot. SERVES 4

Note: Bean sprouts may be omitted.

41

醬
蛋 **Celery and Egg Appetizer**

color—page 37

1 stalk celery
dash of salt
dash of monosodium glutamate
6 hard-boiled eggs
2 star aniseeds or dash of pepper

1 t. sugar
1 t. sesame oil
4 T. soy sauce
4 T. water

Remove tough part of celery, slice diagonally into bite-size pieces and make slits on one edge of each slice. Drop into boiling water, parboil until tender and drain. Sprinkle with salt and monosodium glutamate. Shell eggs and simmer with aniseed, sugar, sesame oil, soy sauce and water for 5 minutes. Let stand 30 minutes, turning occasionally to assure even coloring. Cut eggs into quarters, arrange with celery on serving plate, chill and serve.   SERVES 4

炒
合
包 **Sautéed Vegetables with Omelet**
帶
帽
1/4 lb. lean pork
1 t. wine
1 t. soy sauce
1/2 t. cornstarch
8 T. oil
1/2 cup shredded carrot
1/2 cup shredded mushroom
1/2 cup shredded green pepper
1/2 cup shredded celery
1 1/4 t. salt
1 T. soy sauce
dash of monosodium glutamate
3 eggs

Shred pork and mix with wine, soy sauce and cornstarch. Heat 5 T. oil and sauté over high heat until color changes. Add vegetables and sauté until tender. Season with 1 t. salt, soy sauce and monosodium glutamate, and transfer to serving platter. Beat eggs with 1/4 t. salt, heat 3 T. oil and pour in egg mixture. Tip skillet to spread omelet until large enough to cover vegetables and fry until golden on both sides. Place omelet over vegetables and serve hot.   SERVES 4

燴 Braised Asparagus
龍
須
菜

1 lb. green asparagus
1/8 lb. ham
3 T. oil
2 cups soup stock
1 t. salt
1 t. sugar
1 T. wine
1 T. cornstarch
2 T. water

Remove hard end of asparagus, parboil in salted water and cut into two or three pieces. Slice ham and cut into 1/2″ strips. Heat oil and sauté asparagus over medium heat until coated with oil. Add ham, soup stock, salt, sugar and wine, and bring to a boil. Mix cornstarch and water and add to thicken, stirring constantly. Serve hot.   SERVES 4

蒸 Stuffed Carrot Rolls
胡
蘿
卷

12 lengthwise slices carrot   dash of salt
1 large dried mushroom   dash of monosodium glutamate
2 T. ground chicken   1 T. chopped parsley
2 t. wine   mustard

Cut carrot slices into 2″ × 3″ rectangles, boil until tender, and make 10 slits on one end of each slice. Prepare (Page 19) and slice mushroom into long, thin strips. Mix chicken, wine, salt and monosodium glutamate to make filling. Place 1/4 t. filling on each carrot slice and roll. Garnish with decorative mushroom bands, press unslit end of rolls into parsley, arrange on serving plate and steam over high heat for 10-15 minutes. Serve with mustard.   SERVES 4

鹹 **Pickled Vegetables**
菜 color—page 38

1/2 lb. carrots
1/3 lb. turnips
1/3 lb. cucumbers
1 T. salt
3 T. water
SAUCE:
   3 T. vinegar
   3 t. sugar

Cut vegetables into 2″ lengths and then slice 1/8″ thick and 1 1/2″ wide. Make slits in each slice (Page 22), place in bowl, sprinkle with salt and water and let stand 15 minutes. Wash well, drain and arrange in bowls or dishes. Mix sauce ingredients together and pour over vegetables. Allow sauce to soak in before serving.   SERVES 6

燴 **Braised Lima Beans**
蚕
豆 6 oz. lima beans   SEASONINGS:
2 oz. ham   1 T. wine
10 quail eggs   1 t. salt
1 cup soup stock   1/2 t. sugar
1 t. cornstarch   dash of pepper
2 T. water

Shell lima beans and parboil in salted water. Cut ham to lima-bean size and hard-boil and shell eggs. Bring soup stock to a boil. Add limas, ham, eggs and seasonings, cover and bring to a boil again. Mix cornstarch with water and add to thicken, stirring constantly. Serve hot.   SERVES 4

紅 **Braised Bamboo Shoots and Mushrooms**
燒
筍 1/2 lb. bamboo shoots   4 T. oil
1/2 lb. white mushrooms   1 T. wine

1 t. sugar   1 t. cornstarch
1 t. salt   1 T. water
1 cup soup stock

Slice bamboo shoots and mushrooms into bite-size pieces. Heat oil and sauté over high heat until coated with oil. Add wine, sugar, salt and soup stock and bring to a boil. Mix cornstarch and water and add to thicken, stirring constantly. Serve hot.   SERVES 4

炸冬菇 Fried Mushrooms

18 fresh mushrooms   BATTER:
1/2 t. salt   1 egg white
1/8 t. pepper   2 T. flour
1 T. cornstarch   1 T. water
deep-frying oil

Wash mushrooms in salted water, remove stems, drain, sprinkle with salt and pepper and coat lightly with cornstarch. Stiffly beat egg white and mix with flour, gradually adding water. Add mushrooms to batter, heat oil to 335°F., drop mushrooms in, one by one, and deep fry until golden. Drain on absorbent paper and serve hot.   SERVES 6

魚球湯 Fried-Fish Soup

color—page 37

1/2 lb. white-meat fish   8 cups soup stock
BATTER: 2 t. salt
  1 egg   2 T. wine
  1 T. flour   dash of pepper
  1 T. cornstarch
deep-frying oil

Cut fish into bite-size pieces and beat batter ingredients together. Dip fish in batter, heat oil to 340°F. and deep fry until crisp. Bring soup stock to a boil, add fried fish and remaining ingredients and bring to a second boil. Serve hot.
                                                           SERVES 4

45

全
鶏
湯 **Whole-Chicken Soup**

1 whole spring chicken
1 leek
3 dried mushrooms
5 slices ginger
5 slices bamboo shoot
5 leaves spinach or other leafy green vegetable
1 T. salt
3 T. wine
dash of pepper

Dress chicken, cut leek into 2″ lengths, and prepare (Page 19) and slice mush‚
rooms. Place chicken, ginger and leek in a potful of water, bring to a boil
and simmer for 30 minutes. Arrange vegetables over chicken, add remaining
ingredients, simmer 10 more minutes and serve.   SERVES 6

菠
菜
蛋
花
湯 **Egg Flower Soup with Spinach**

2 bunches young spinach
5 cups soup stock
1 cup sliced bamboo shoot
2 t. salt
dash of pepper
dash of monosodium glutamate
2 eggs
1 T. wine

Parboil spinach in salted water and cut into 1 1/2″ lengths. Bring soup stock to
a boil, add bamboo shoot and season with salt, pepper and monosodium
glutamate. Beat eggs lightly, bring stock to a boil again and pour in eggs, stirring
slowly. Add spinach and wine and serve hot.   SERVES 4

46

SUMMER

Chicken and Green Pepper Appetizer
Chicken with Peppers
Sweet-and-Sour Fish
Sautéed Fish with Tomato
Shrimp with Green Peppers and Mushrooms
Braised Abalone and Cucumber
Crab with Braised Eggplant
Fried Scallops
Sautéed Frog Legs
Jellied Beef
Sautéed Beef and Green Peppers
Braised Curry Beef
Assorted Meatballs
Sweet-and-Sour Meatballs
Meatballs with Sweet Corn
Sweet-and-Sour Pork
Spareribs with Sweet Kumquats
Szechwan Pork
Sweet-and-Sour Sauce Eggs
Scrambled Eggs with Green Pepper
Scrambled Eggs and Tomato
Stuffed Eggplant
Stuffed Green Peppers
Chilled Bean Sprouts
Fruit and Vegetable Salad
Pork, Cucumber, and Vermicelli Salad
Bright Vegetable Salad
Braised Vegetables
Braised Pumpkin
Sliced-Chicken Soup
Chicken-Ball Soup
Egg Flower Soup

白切鷄 Chicken and Green Pepper Appetizer

1/2 chicken	4 T. wine
1 leek	2 t. salt
1 star aniseed	4 green peppers
1 t. black peppercorns	soy sauce
4 slices ginger	sesame oil
2 t. sesame oil	monosodium glutamate

Clean chicken and cut leek into 2″ lengths. Place aniseed and peppercorns in small cloth bag so that they can be easily discarded after use. Place chicken, leek, bagged spices and ginger in a half-full pot of water, cover and bring to a boil. Lower heat, move lid slightly to allow steam to escape and simmer 30 minutes. Remove chicken and pour cold water over it to cool quickly. Dry with a cloth, brush with sesame oil and rub with wine and salt. Bone and slice. Wash green peppers and dry with a cloth. Bake in slow oven or cook over open fire until brown. Rub away thin skin with a cheesecloth, halve, seed and slice. Arrange chicken and green pepper on serving dish and serve cold. Sprinkle with soy sauce, sesame oil and monosodium glutamate to taste. SERVES 4

辣子鷄 Chicken with Peppers

1/2 spring chicken	3 slices ginger
1 T. wine	1 T. wine
1 T. soy sauce	1 t. sugar
3 T. cornstarch	2 T. soy sauce
deep-frying oil	dash of monosodium
3 green peppers	glutamate
2 red peppers	2 t. cornstarch
1 clove garlic	1/2 cup water
3 T. oil	

Clean and cut chicken into bite-size pieces. Sprinkle with wine and soy sauce and coat with cornstarch. Heat oil to 340°F. and deep fry until crisp. Quarter and seed green peppers. Halve and seed red peppers. Crush garlic clove. Heat oil and sauté red peppers, ginger and garlic over high heat for 1 minute. Add green peppers and sauté until coated with oil. Add fried chicken, wine, sugar, soy sauce and monosodium glutamate and bring to a boil. Mix cornstarch with water and add to thicken. SERVES 4

糖
醋
全
魚

Sweet-and-Sour Fish

color—page 57

1 whole white-meat fish	1/3 cup diced carrot
(about 1 1/2 lb.)	1/3 cup diced bamboo shoot
deep-frying oil	1 T. cornstarch
3 T. oil	1/2 cup water
1/3 cup diced green pepper	MIXTURE B:
MIXTURE A:	6 T. sugar
2 T. wine	3 T. vinegar
2 T. soy sauce	1 T. soy sauce
3 T. cornstarch	1 T. tomato sauce
3 T. flour	1 t. salt

Clean and scale fish and make 3 diagonal slashes on each side. Rub well inside and out with *Mixture A*. Heat oil to 330°F. and deep fry until crisp and golden brown (about 15 minutes), basting often with hot oil. Remove to absorbent paper and drain. Flatten stomach slightly to make fish stand as shown in color photograph and place in a slow oven to keep warm. Heat oil and sauté green pepper, carrot and bamboo shoot over high heat until tender. Add *Mixture B* and bring to a boil. Mix cornstarch with water and add to thicken, stirring constantly. Pour over fish and serve hot.   SERVES 4-6

蕃
茄
魚
片

Sautéed Fish with Tomato

3/4 lb. white-meat fish
1 egg white
2 t. cornstarch
deep-frying oil
1 medium tomato
2 T. oil
1 T. tomato catsup
1/2 t. salt
1/2 t. sugar
2 t. cornstarch
1 T. water
1 t. sesame oil

Cut fish into bite-size pieces and mix with egg white and cornstarch. Heat oil to 320°F. and deep fry fish. Remove quickly before it turns brown. Dip tomato

50

in boiling water, peel away skin and slice. Heat oil and sauté tomato over high heat for two minutes. Add tomato catsup, salt, sugar and fish. Mix cornstarch with water and add to thicken, stirring constantly. Flavor with sesame oil before removing from heat. Serve hot.   SERVES 4

炒青椒蝦仁 Shrimp with Green Peppers and Mushrooms

1/2 lb. shrimp
1/2 t. ginger juice
1 t. cornstarch
5 T. oil
1/2 cup diced white mushrooms
1/2 cup diced green peppers
1 t. salt
1 t. sugar
2 t. wine

Shell and devein shrimps, sprinkle with ginger juice and cornstarch and let stand 5 minutes. Heat oil and sauté over high heat until color changes. Add mushrooms and green peppers and cook until tender. Add remaining ingredients, stir for a few minutes and serve hot.   SERVES 2

鮑魚黃瓜条 Braised Abalone and Cucumber

3 canned abalones
1 lb. cucumbers
3 T. oil
1 t. salt
1/2 t. sugar
1 cup soup stock
2 t. cornstarch
2 T. water

Cut abalones into 3/4″ × 2 1/2″ strips and half-slice (Page 22). Peel cucumbers and cut in same way. Heat oil and sauté abalone until coated with oil. Add cucumber, salt, sugar and soup stock and cook over medium heat for 5 minutes. Mix cornstarch with water and add to thicken. Serve hot.   SERVES 4

蟹粉茄子 Crab with Braised Eggplant

4 oz. canned crab meat	1/2 t. salt
5-6 eggplants (about 3 oz. each)	2 t. sugar
deep-frying oil	1 T. wine
2 T. oil	1 t. soy sauce
1/2 t. grated ginger	

Drain crab meat, remove filaments and separate into small pieces. Remove stems from eggplants, peel, slice vertically, 1/2″ thick, soak in water 10 minutes to prevent discoloring and drain well. Heat oil to 335°F., deep fry eggplant until slightly brown and remove to plate. Heat oil and sauté crab meat and ginger over medium heat for 2 minutes. Add fried eggplant and remaining ingredients, and cook over medium heat for 5 minutes.   SERVES 4

炸鮮貝 Fried Scallops

10 fresh scallops	1/2 t. salt
1/2 t. ginger juice	3 T. flour
1 egg	1/4 t. baking powder
1 t. wine	deep-frying oil

Wash scallops in salted water, remove thin skins, cut into bite-size pieces, parboil, drain and sprinkle with ginger juice. Beat egg, blend with wine, salt, flour and baking powder and mix with scallops. Heat oil to 335°F., deep fry until golden and serve hot.   SERVES 4

炒田鷄腿 Sautéed Frog Legs

1 lb. frog legs
1 T. wine
1 t. cornstarch
deep-frying oil
2 T. oil
1/2 cup diced green pepper
1/2 cup 1″ celery wedges
2 T. soy sauce
1/2 t. sugar

52

Cut frog legs into bite-size pieces, sprinkle with wine and cornstarch and let stand 5 minutes. Heat oil to 330°F., deep fry until color changes slightly and drain. Heat oil and sauté green pepper and celery until well coated with oil. Add frog legs and remaining ingredients, heat well and transfer to serving dish.

SERVES 4

五香牛凍 Jellied Beef

1/2 lb. beef tenderloin	1 t. black peppercorns
2 slices cucumber	2 star aniseeds
2 slices carrot	1 T. soy sauce
2 T. powdered gelatin	1/2 t. salt
4 T. water	1/2 t. sugar
1/2 leek	1 T. wine

Cut beef into chunks. Cut cucumber and carrot into flower shapes. Mix gelatin with water and set aside. Place beef and remaining ingredients in a pot with 5 cups of water, bring to a boil and simmer for 30 minutes. Remove beef and strain 2 cups of liquid. Mix liquid with gelatin mixture and stir to thoroughly dissolve gelatin. Separate beef into small shreds and mix with gelatin mixture. Arrange cucumber and carrot in a mold, pour in 1/4 of beef-gelatin mixture and cool until partially set. Pour in remaining mixture and chill. Invert on chilled plate and serve.

SERVES 4

青椒牛肉糸 Sautéed Beef and Green Peppers

1 lb. beef	7 T. oil
1/4 lb. bamboo shoots	2 cups shredded green pepper
MARINADE:	1 T. wine
1/2 egg white	1 1/2 T. soy sauce
1 T. wine	1 1/2 t. sugar
1 T. soy sauce	1/2 t. salt
1 t. cornstarch	

Shred beef and bamboo shoots. Mix marinade ingredients and marinate beef for 5 minutes. Heat 4 T. oil and sauté beef over high heat until color changes. Set aside. Heat 3 T. oil and sauté bamboo shoots and green pepper over high heat until coated with oil. Add beef and remaining ingredients, stir 1 minute and serve hot.

SERVES 4

咖
哩
牛
肉
Braised Curry Beef

2 1/2 lbs. beef
1 lb. potatoes
1/2 lb. onions
4 cloves garlic
5 T. oil
2 T. curry powder

1 T. salt
2 T. wine
deep-frying oil
1 T. cornstarch
3 T. water

Cut beef and potatoes into 1 1/2″ cubes. Dip beef in hot water and drain. Soak potatoes in water for 5 minutes and dry. Cut onions into eighths and crush garlic cloves. Heat oil and sauté onion and garlic over high heat for a few minutes. Add curry powder and stir well. Add beef, salt, wine and enough water to cover. Lower heat, cover and simmer until tender (about 2 hours). Heat oil to 335°F., and deep fry potatoes until slightly brown. Add potatoes to beef and continue cooking 5 minutes. Arrange onion, beef and potato on serving platter and heat remaining liquid. Mix cornstarch with water and add to thicken. Pour over braised beef and vegetables and serve hot. SERVES 8

肉
丸
子
Assorted Meatballs
color—page 58

1 lb. ground pork
1 T. chopped leek
1/2 t. grated garlic
1 egg
1 T. wine
1 t. salt
1 T. soy sauce
1 T. sesame oil
2 T. cornstarch
2 T. flour
1/2 cup glutinuous rice
1 egg
1 egg yolk
deep-frying oil
1/3 lb. snow peas

2 T. oil
dash of salt
dash of monosodium glutamate
red pepper oil (Page 25)
salt mixture (Page 25)

Mix the first 10 ingredients well and form into small balls (about 30). Uniform-size balls can be easily made using a tablespoon (see process photograph).

54

1. Pearl Meatballs: Roll 10 meatballs in glutinous rice that has been soaked in water for 3 hours and well drained. Steam for 40 minutes.

2. Golden Meatballs: Beat egg and egg yolk with a dash of salt. Grease heated skillet and pour in enough egg mixture to thinly coat bottom of skillet. When egg sets, remove. Repeat process until all the egg is used. Shred egg sheets and strew over 10 meatballs. Steam 15 minutes.

3. Deep-fried Meatballs: Heat oil to 360°F. and deep fry remaining meatballs until golden brown, gradually lowering heat to medium. Drain on absorbent paper.

String snow peas, heat oil, add salt and sauté snow peas over high heat for 1 minute. Sprinkle with monosodium glutamate. Arrange three meatball varieties on serving plate with snow peas and serve hot with red pepper oil and salt mixture.

SERVES 4

Note: Adding salt to oil before sautéing snow peas guarantees a fresher, greener color. Try this trick with all your sautéed green vegetable dishes.

糖
醋
肉
丸

Sweet-and-Sour Meatballs

color—page 58

1 lb. ground pork
1 T. chopped leek or onion
1/2 t. grated garlic
1 egg
1 T. wine
1 t. salt
1 T. soy sauce
1 T. sesame oil
2 T. cornstarch
2 T. flour
deep-frying oil
1 T. oil

1/2 cup bite-size green pepper wedges
SAUCE:
  5 T. sugar
  4 T. vinegar
  3 T. soy sauce
  1/2 t. salt
  1 t. wine
  1/2 cup soup stock or water
1 1/2 T. cornstarch
1 1/2 cups water
1 cup chunk-style pineapple

Mix the first 10 ingredients well and form into small balls. Heat oil to 360°F. and deep fry over medium heat until brown. Heat oil and sauté green pepper over high heat for 1 minute. Heat sauce ingredients in saucepan and bring to a boil. Mix cornstarch with water and add to thicken. Add meatballs, green pepper and pineapple. Serve hot.

SERVES 4

粟
米
肉
丸 **Meatballs with Sweet Corn**

1 lb. ground pork
1 T. chopped leek
1/2 t. ginger juice
1/2 t. grated garlic
1 egg
1 T. wine
1 t. salt
1 T. soy sauce
1 t. sesame oil
2 T. cornstarch
deep-frying oil
1 1/2 cups canned sweet corn
1 cup broth or water
2 t. cornstarch
2 T. water

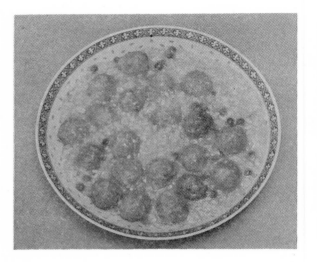

Mix the first 10 ingredients together and form into small balls. Heat oil to 330°F., deep fry until brown and drain well. Heat sweet corn and broth and bring to a boil. Mix cornstarch with water and add to thicken, stirring constantly. Bring to a boil again, add meatballs, mix, and serve hot.   SERVES 4

July 7 is a holiday celebrating the legendary story▶ of the cowherd and the weaver who were so engrossed in their love that they forgot their work. This irresponsibility angered the King of Heaven who forbade them to meet again. Seeing the grief of the lovers, the god relented and sent a magpie to tell them that they might meet on the seventh day of each week. The messenger, however, stammered and repeated "seven" twice and the lovers thought that they could meet only on the seventh day of the seventh month of each year. The soup shown here has been prepared especially for this occasion, with lily buds that are traditionally eaten on this festival day and carrot slices cut in heart shapes. *Clockwise from the top:* Sliced-Chicken Soup (Page 65), Sweet-and-Sour Fish (Page 50), Spareribs with Sweet Kumquats, and Szechwan Pork (Page 60).

糖
醋
肉

Sweet-and-Sour Pork

1 lb. lean pork
1 T. wine
2 T. soy sauce
1 carrot (4 oz.)
3 green peppers
1 onion (4 oz.)
2 slices canned pineapple
1 egg
2 T. flour
1 T. cornstarch
deep-frying oil
5 T. oil
1 T. cornstarch
1/2 cup water

SAUCE:
6 T. sugar
4 T. soy sauce
1 T. wine
2 T. vinegar
4 T. tomato puree

Cut pork into bite-size pieces and marinate in wine and soy sauce for 15 minutes. Cut carrot into bite-size wedges, parboil for 8 minutes and drain. Seed green peppers and cut into bite-size wedges. Cut onion and pineapple into bite-size wedges. Beat egg lightly with flour and cornstarch, dip pork in mixture, heat oil to 330°F. and deep fry until golden brown and crisp. Set aside. Mix sauce ingredients together. Heat oil and sauté carrot, peppers, and onion over high heat for 2 minutes. Add sauce and bring to a boil. Mix cornstarch and water and add to thicken, stirring constantly. Add fried pork and pineapple, mix well and serve hot. SERVES 4

◄ *Top to bottom:* Assorted Meatballs (Page 54), Sweet-and-Sour Meatballs (Page 55), and Chicken-Ball Soup (Page 66).

排骨金橘 **Spareribs with Sweet Kumquats**

color—page 57

2 lbs. spareribs	SAUCE:
1 T. wine	1 T. wine
1 T. soy sauce	2 T. sugar
1 t. ginger juice	2 1/2 T. soy sauce
1 T. cornstarch	1 1/2 T. vinegar
deep-frying oil	1/2 t. salt
1 T. oil	1 t. cornstarch
1 T. chopped leek	dash of monosodium glutamate
1 T. chopped ginger	2 T. water
1 1/2 cups sweet kumquats (Page 105)	

Cut spareribs into 2″-3″ lengths and marinate in wine, soy sauce and ginger juice for 20 minutes. Coat spareribs with cornstarch, heat oil to 360°F. and deep fry for 10 minutes or until brown. Heat oil and sauté leek and ginger over high heat for 1 minute. Mix sauce ingredients and add, stirring constantly. When sauce thickens, add fried spareribs. Arrange on plate with sweet kumquats and serve hot.   SERVES 6

雲白肉 **Szechwan Pork**

color page—57

1 lb. pork rump	1 T. toasted and grated sesame seeds
1 leek	1/2 t. grated garlic
7 slices ginger	2 T. chopped onion or leek
1/2 cup shredded cucumber	
2 T. sesame oil	
2 T. chopped red pepper	
2 T. soy sauce	
1/2 t. sugar	
1 T. vinegar	
1/2 t. salt	

Tie pork tightly with string and cut leek into 2″ lengths. Boil pork, leek and 5 slices ginger over high heat until tender (about 45 minutes). Remove and let cool. Cut very thin and arrange on serving plate with shredded cucumber. Heat sesame oil and sauté red pepper and 2 slices ginger. When pepper turns light brown, remove it and ginger and discard. Add soy sauce, sugar, vinegar, salt and sesame seeds and bring to a boil. Remove from heat and let cool. Mix with garlic and onion, pour over sliced pork and serve cold.   SERVES 4

糖 醋 合 包 蛋 Sweet-and-Sour Sauce Eggs

6 T. oil

6 eggs

SAUCE:

   3 T. sugar

   2 T. soy sauce

   1 1/2 T. vinegar

   2 T. tomato catsup

   1 T. cornstarch

   1/2 cup water

Heat 1 T. oil in a large, shallow metal ladle and break one egg into it. Fry over low heat until edges are set and turn over gently with a fork. Fry other side until white is completely cooked. Remove to platter. Repeat process with remaining five eggs. Heat sauce ingredients, stirring constantly until thickened. Pour sauce over eggs and serve hot.   SERVES 6

Variation: Add a chopped leek and 2 t. red pepper oil (Page 25) to sauce.

青 椒 炒 蛋 Scrambled Eggs with Green Pepper

4 eggs

1/2 t. salt

dash of monosodium glutamate

1/2 cup diced green pepper

4 T. oil

Beat eggs lightly with salt and monosodium glutamate and mix with green pepper. Heat oil and scramble mixture over high heat until eggs are half-done. Serve hot.   SERVES 2

61

蕃茄炒蛋 Scrambled Eggs and Tomato

1 tomato	1/2 t. salt
4 eggs	5 T. oil

Dip tomato in boiling water, peel away skin, cut into bite-size pieces and remove seeds. Beat eggs with salt, heat oil and scramble until half-done. Add tomato and stir over medium heat for 2 minutes. SERVES 2

Note: Another way to peel a tomato is to spear with a fork and hold over gas flame, turning so that all sides are exposed. The skin will slip off easily.

炸茄盒 Stuffed Eggplant

1 lb. small eggplants
FILLING:
    1/2 lb. ground pork
    1/2 t. grated ginger
    1 T. chopped leek
    2 t. soy sauce
    1/2 t. salt
    1 t. wine
    dash of monosodium glutamate
1 egg
1/2 cup water
1/2 t. salt
1 cup flour

deep-frying oil
salt mixture (Page 25)
tomato catsup

Peel eggplants, remove stems and soak in water 20 minutes to prevent discoloring. Slice 1/4" thick and make a slit in each slice. Combine filling ingredients and mix well. Stuff slits in eggplant slices. Beat egg with water, salt and flour and dip stuffed eggplant into mixture. Heat oil to 330°F. and deep fry until golden brown. Serve hot with salt mixture or tomato catsup. SERVES 4

肉釀青椒 Stuffed Green Peppers

4 green peppers
1/2 lb. ground pork

62

1 egg
1 T. wine
2 T. soy sauce
dash of monosodium glutamate
3 T. oil
1 cup water
1 t. salt
2 t. cornstarch
1/2 cup water

Halve green peppers vertically and remove seeds. Mix pork, egg, wine, soy sauce and monosodium glutamate, divide into 8 portions and stuff each pepper half with one portion. Heat oil and sauté both sides of peppers, meat side first, over low heat until brown. Add water and salt and bring to a boil. Mix cornstarch with water and add to thicken. Serve hot.   SERVES 4

凉拌豆芽菜 Chilled Bean Sprouts

12 oz. bean sprouts   *1 T. vinegar*
1 T. sesame oil   *dash of monosodium glutamate*
2 T. soy sauce

Remove both ends of bean sprouts, parboil, drain and cool. (If using canned sprouts, rinse in fresh water and drain.) Mix remaining ingredients for dressing and pour over sprouts just before serving.   SERVES 4

拌中西菜果 Fruit and Vegetable Salad

1 head cauliflower
1 head broccoli
3 small tomatoes
20 canned or fresh cherries
20 canned or fresh litchi

Separate cauliflower and broccoli into flowerets, parboil and arrange on serving plate with broccoli over cauliflower. Thinly slice tomatoes and arrange around edge of cauliflower. Alternating litchis and cherries, make another ring around edge of tomato. Serve cold with favorite dressing (Page 25).   SERVES 6

拌
黄
瓜
粉
糸

Pork, Cucumber, and Vermicelli Salad

1/2 lb. pork
1 lb. cucumbers
1/8 lb. transparent vermicelli
2 t. soy sauce
2 t. wine
1 t. cornstarch
3 T. oil
1/2 cup shredded leek

Shred pork and cucumbers. Soak vermicelli in hot water for 20 minutes and cut into 2″ lengths. Marinate pork in soy sauce, wine and cornstarch for 5 minutes. Heat oil and sauté over high heat until tender. Arrange cucumber on bottom of serving plate, place vermicelli over cucumber, pork over vermicelli, and leek over pork. Serve cold with favorite Chinese dressing (Page 25).   SERVES 4

拌
蔬
菜

Bright Vegetable Salad

1 1/2 cups shredded red cabbage
1 1/2 cups shredded cucumber
1 1/2 cups shredded green pepper
1 1/2 cups shredded radish
1 1/2 cups shredded carrot

Arrange vegetables attractively on serving plate according to color. (Photograph arrangement: cabbage in the center, surrounded by carrot, cucumber, pepper and radish.) Vary the order until you find your favorite arrangement. Serve cold with favorite dressing (Page 25).   SERVES 4

Note: If you slice cucumbers diagonally, then shred, each shred will have a spot of dark green skin on either end.

64

燴什錦 Braised Vegetables

2 small eggplants
2 green peppers
2 potatoes
2 onions
1 tomato
1 clove garlic

3 T. oil
1 T. wine
1 t. salt
1/2 t. sugar
2 T. soy sauce

Cut vegetables into bite-size pieces and set aside. Crush garlic, heat oil and sauté over high heat until brown. Add eggplants, potatoes and onions and sauté for 3 minutes. Add wine, salt, sugar and soy sauce, lower heat, cover and simmer until tender. Add tomato and green peppers and continue cooking 5 minutes. Serve hot.   SERVES 4

燉南瓜 Braised Pumpkin

1 lb. pumpkin
1/2 leek
4 T. oil
1/2 t. salt
1/4 t. sugar
1/2 cup water

Peel and cut pumpkin into bite-size pieces and chop leek. Heat oil and sauté pumpkin over high heat until coated with oil. Add leek and remaining ingredients, cover and cook until tender (about 15 minutes). Serve hot.   SERVES 4

鶏片湯 Sliced-Chicken Soup

color—page 57

1/4 lb. chicken meat
1 t. cornstarch
dash of salt
dash of monosodium glutamate
12 dried lily buds
8 slices carrot

1/4 lb. spinach or other leafy green
   vegetable
6 cups soup stock
1 1/2 t. salt
1 T. wine
1 egg

65

Slice chicken meat very thin and sprinkle with cornstarch, salt and mono-sodium glutamate. Prepare dried lily buds (Page 18) and drain. Cut carrot slices into heart shapes and parboil. Wash, separate and parboil spinach. Heat soup stock, add chicken and bring to a boil. Add salt, wine, lily buds, carrot and spinach. Beat egg lightly and add slowly, stirring as you pour. Serve hot.

SERVES 4

鶏
丸 **Chicken-Ball Soup**
湯 color—page 58

1/2 lb. ground chicken meat   3/4 lb. small cucumbers
1 egg white   7 cups soup stock
2 t. wine   1 3/4 t. salt
3/4 t. salt
2 t. sesame oil
1 T. cornstarch

Mix the first 6 ingredients together well and form into small balls. Cut cucumber into 4″ lengths and slice thinly. Bring soup stock to a boil and gently drop in chicken balls. When balls float to surface, add cucumber and remaining season-ings, bring to a boil again and serve hot.

SERVES 4

蕃
茄
蛋 **Egg Flower Soup**
花
湯 2 tomatoes   1 T. wine
1 egg   1 t. salt
1 onion   dash of pepper
3 T. oil
6 cups soup stock

Dip tomatoes in boiling water, peel away skins and cut each into eighths. Beat egg lightly and set aside. Cut onion into eighths, heat oil and sauté until golden. Add tomato and remaining ingredients and bring to a boil. Gradually pour in egg, stirring soup with a few sweeping motions as you pour. Serve hot.

SERVES 4

66

AUTUMN

Fried Chicken with Cashews
Chicken with Chestnuts
Beggar's Chicken
Chicken Puffs
Silver Dollar Chicken
Soy-Sauce Chicken
Liver-and-Bacon Rolls
Crisp Fried Fish
Fish with Sweet-and-Sour Sauce
Sautéed Shrimp with Broccoli
Shrimp Toast
Steamed Crab
Fried Crab Balls
Squid with Green Peppers and Mushrooms
Beef with Oyster Sauce
Beef Tenderloin and Mushrooms
Sautéed Beef with Leek
Sautéed Beef with Bean Paste
Sliced Mutton with Peppers
Deep-Fried Mutton
Chilled Pork Kidney with Carrot
Braised Pork Tripe
Braised Pork with Radish
Peking-Style Eggs
Scrambled Eggs with Spinach
Chinese Cabbage with Chestnuts
Tangy Chinese Cabbage
Braised Cauliflower
Bean Curd with Shrimp and Chicken
Spinach Salad
Cream Soup with Cabbage

炒腰果鶏丁 Fried Chicken with Cashews

1 lb. chicken
1 egg white
2 t. cornstarch
1 cup cashew nuts
deep-frying oil
1 leek
6 T. oil
2 slices ginger
1 cup peeled, wedged cucumber
1 T. wine   2 T. soy sauce
1 t. sugar   1 T. water

Bone chicken and cut into 1/2" cubes. Mix with egg white and 1 t. cornstarch. Blanch cashew nuts, heat oil to 320°F. and deep fry until golden brown, stirring constantly. Nuts burn easily, so remove as soon as color changes and drain. Cut leek into 1/2" lengths, heat oil and sauté leek and ginger with chicken and cucumber until chicken turns white. Add wine, sugar and soy sauce. Mix 1 t. cornstarch with water and add to thicken. Add fried cashew nuts, mix well and serve hot.   SERVES 4

炒栗子鶏丁 Chicken with Chestnuts

1 lb. chicken fillet
2 t. wine
1 t. cornstarch
1 egg white
8 T. oil
1/2 cup cubed green pepper
1/2 cup cubed chestnuts (canned)
1/2 t. sugar
1 t. salt

Cube chicken fillet and mix with wine, cornstarch and egg white. Heat 5 T. oil and sauté over high heat until color changes. Set aside. Heat 3 T. oil and sauté green peppers and chestnuts over high heat for 2-3 minutes. Add chicken and remaining ingredients, stir well and serve hot.   SERVES 4

叫
化
鶏
Beggar's Chicken

color—page 78

1 spring chicken
2 t. salt
1 T. sesame oil
1 t. ground black peppercorns
2 T. wine
1/4 lb. pork
3 T. oil
6 T. chopped leek or onion
2 cups chopped pickled beets
1 T. soy sauce
2-3 large dried lotus leaves
string (about 10 feet)
clay

Dress and wash chicken and rub inside and out with salt, sesame oil, ground peppercorns and wine. Shred pork, heat oil and sauté pork, leek and pickled beets over medium heat until tender. Add soy sauce. Soak lotus leaves in hot water until tender, stuff chicken with sautéed ingredients, wrap with lotus leaves and tie with string. Mix clay with water and knead to consistency of soft dough. Cover wrapped chicken with a 1/2″ clay coating and bake at 350°F. for 1 hour. Lower heat to 200°F. and continue baking another hour. To serve, crack clay shell and remove both shell and lotus leaves. SERVES 4-6

Note: Foil may be substituted for lotus leaves, and flour for clay. If chicken is to be stuffed well in advance of baking, stuffing should be allowed to cool first. Clay should be applied just before baking.

烤
紙
包
鶏
Chicken Puffs

color—page 78

1/2 lb. spring chicken (with skin)
8 slices ginger
8 slices mushroom
8 slices onion or leek
2 T. wine
2 T. soy sauce
4 10″ squares waxed paper

4 3" *squares foil*
2 *egg whites*
dash of salt

Slice chicken into 8 pieces. Marinate chicken, ginger, mushroom and onion in wine and soy sauce for 10 minutes. Spread waxed paper, fold foil in half, and place in center. Put two slices of each marinated ingredient on foil and twist edges of waxed paper to close. Beat egg whites stiffly with salt and brush over waxed paper. Repeat process to make four chicken puffs. Place in slow oven and bake until chicken is tender (about 15 minutes).   SERVES 4

Note: If powdered calcium is added to the egg whites they will be a strong, clear white color and the puffs will be far more attractive when served. (Powdered calcium can be found at your pharmacy.)

芙
蓉
鶏
片
Silver Dollar Chicken

1/4 lb. chicken fillet
6 T. water
1 t. wine
1 1/2 t. salt
2 T. cornstarch
6 stiffly beaten egg whites
deep-frying oil
6 snow peas
1/2 cup button mushrooms
3 slices ham
2 T. chicken fat
1 cup soup stock
dash of monosodium glutamate

Mince chicken fillet, adding 3 T. water. Mix with wine, 1/2 t. salt, and 1 T. cornstarch and fold into beaten egg whites. Heat oil to 320°F., pour the chicken mixture into the oil, little by little, from a small ladle to form "coins" and deep fry over low heat so they do not brown. As soon as they float to the surface, remove to a plate. String snow peas, slice mushrooms and cut ham into diamond shapes. Heat chicken fat and sauté snow peas, mushrooms and ham over high heat for 1 minute. Add soup stock, monosodium glutamate and 1 t. salt and bring to a boil. Mix 1 T. cornstarch with 3 T. water and add to thicken. Pour sauce over chicken "coins" and serve hot.   SERVES 4

醬
油
鶏 **Soy-Sauce Chicken**

1 spring chicken, dressed | 4 slices ginger
1 t. black pepper | 5 T. soy sauce
1 t. salt | 3 T. sesame oil
4 T. wine | 1 T. sugar
1 leek | parsley

Rub chicken, inside and out, with black pepper, salt and 3 T. wine. Cut leek into 4″ lengths. Stuff chicken with leek and ginger, place in bowl and steam over high heat for 30 minutes. Reserve liquid. Heat soy sauce, sesame oil, sugar, 1 T. wine and 1 cup of liquid from steamed chicken. Add chicken and continue cooking until brown, turning occasionally. Garnish with parsley.

SERVES 4

炸
鶏
肝 **Liver-and-Bacon Rolls**
卷
1/2 lb. chicken livers
1 T. wine
1 T. chopped leek
1 T. soy sauce
15 water chestnuts
15 4″ lengths of bacon
deep-frying oil

Cut livers into bite-size pieces, wash well to remove blood and drain. Marinate in wine, leek and soy sauce for 10 minutes, remove and dry carefully with a cloth. Place one piece of liver and one chestnut on each bacon slice, roll and secure with a toothpick. Heat oil to 335°F. and deep fry until crisp. Serve hot or cold as an appetizer.

SERVES 6

香
酥
魚 **Crisp Fried Fish**

6 small fish
1/2 cup soy sauce
1/2 T. wine
1 star aniseed
6 slices ginger

deep-frying oil
1/2 cup shredded leek

Clean and scale fish and marinate in soy sauce, wine, star aniseed and ginger for 30 minutes. Remove and wipe well. Heat oil to 335°F. and deep fry until crisp. Arrange on platter and garnish with leek. Serve hot or cold.   SERVES 6

澆汁酥魚 Fish with Sweet-and-Sour Sauce

8 small fish
1/2 cup soy sauce
1/2 T. wine
1 star aniseed
6 slices ginger
deep-frying oil
2 T. oil
1/2 cup wedged leek
2 T. sugar
2 T. vinegar

1 T. soy sauce
2 t. cornstarch
1/2 cup water

Clean and scale fish and marinate in soy sauce, wine, star aniseed and ginger for 30 minutes. Remove and wipe well. Heat oil to 330°F. and deep fry until crisp. Heat oil and sauté leek over high heat until tender. Add sugar, vinegar and soy sauce and bring to a boil. Mix cornstarch with water and add to thicken, stirring constantly. Arrange fried fish on serving platter, pour sauce over fish and serve hot.   SERVES 4

蝦仁炒芥蘭菜 Sautéed Shrimp with Broccoli

1 lb. shrimp
1/2 t. ginger juice
2 t. cornstarch
1 head broccoli
5 T. oil
1 t. salt
1 t. sugar
2 t. wine
1 T. water

Shell and devein shrimps and remove tails. Mix with ginger juice and 1 t. cornstarch and let stand 5 minutes. Separate broccoli into flowerets and parboil. Heat oil and sauté shrimps over high heat until color changes. Add broccoli, salt, sugar and wine and continue cooking until coated with oil. Mix 1 t. cornstarch with water and add to thicken, stirring constantly. Serve hot.   SERVES 4

蝦仁吐司 Shrimp Toast

3/4 lb. shrimp
6 T. water
1 egg white
1 t. ginger juice
1 t. salt
1 t. wine
1 t. cornstarch
7 slices bread
7 hard-boiled quail eggs
parsley
deep-frying oil

Shell and mince shrimps, adding water, and mix with egg white, ginger juice, salt, wine and cornstarch. Remove bread crusts and halve slices; shell and halve quail eggs. Spread each piece of bread with shrimp mixture and garnish with quail-egg halves and parsley, pressing down lightly to make garnish adhere. Heat oil to 330°F., gently drop in bread with shrimp-spread side down, and deep fry until bread browns slightly. Drain on absorbent paper and serve hot.

SERVES 4-6

蒸青蟹 Steamed Crab

color—page 77

2 fresh crabs
1 T. vinegar
1 t. ginger juice

1 t. wine
1 T. soy sauce
1 t. sugar

Wash crabs in cold running water to remove all sand. Steam over high heat for 25 minutes or until shells turn red. Mix remaining ingredients for dip. Serve crabs hot or cold with dip and with shell crackers.   SERVES 4

Note: Crabs are most succulent during the chrysanthemum season, and in China guests were often invited to appreciate the flowers, compose poetry and enjoy crabs. The dish is enhanced when served with rice and hot wine. (Chrysanthemum leaves are useful in removing fish odors from the hands).

炸蟹丸子 Fried Crab Balls

2 eggs
1/2 lb. crab meat (canned or fresh)
2 T. chopped leek
1 cup flour
1 t. baking powder
1/2 t. salt
1 T. oil
deep-frying oil
salt mixture (Page 25)

Beat eggs and mix well with crab meat, leek, flour, baking powder, salt and oil. Form into small balls with a tablespoon (Page 54). Heat oil to 335°F. and deep fry until golden brown. Drain on absorbent paper and serve hot with salt mixture.

SERVES 4

炒魷魚 Squid with Green Peppers and Mushrooms

color—page 77

3 squid
1 T. wine
1/2 t. ginger juice
1 t. cornstarch
deep-frying oil

3 green peppers
1/2 cup canned mushrooms
3 T. oil
1 t. salt

Cut squid open, remove legs, center bones and thin skins from both sides and clean well. Score each squid on one side in a crisscross pattern and cut into bite-size pieces. Sprinkle with wine, ginger juice and cornstarch, heat oil to 320°F. and deep fry for a moment. Do not allow to brown. Seed green peppers and cut into bite-size pieces. Make slits on peppers and mushrooms, heat oil and sauté over high heat for 2 minutes. Add squid, season with salt and serve hot.

SERVES 4

炒
蠔
油
牛
肉

Beef with Oyster Sauce

1 lb. beef
2 T. soy sauce
1 T. wine
1 t. cornstarch
5 T. oil
2 T. canned oyster sauce
1 t. sugar
16 canned chestnuts

Cut beef into bite-size pieces and marinate in soy sauce, wine and cornstarch for 5 minutes. Heat oil and sauté over high heat until color changes. Add oyster sauce and sugar and mix well. Serve hot, garnished with chestnuts.   SERVES 4

The moon is thought to be most beautiful on the ▶ fifteenth day of the eighth month according to the old Chinese calendar. Moon-viewing parties are held where people enjoy chrysanthemums, poetry and moon cakes. During the Yüan dynasty when the Mongols controlled China, armed guards were placed among the people and one cooking knife was tied to a well in a central location to be shared by ten families. The Mongols hoped to protect themselves against rebellions in this way. The Chinese knew that they must attack suddenly and simultaneously if they were to overwhelm the armed guards. Small pieces of cloth on which the date of the planned attack had been written were placed in moon cakes and distributed widely. The successful attack was on August 15. *From top to bottom:* Chilled Pork Kidney with Carrot (Page 81), Squid with **Green** Peppers and Mushrooms (Page 75), Steamed Crab (Page 74), and Moon Cakes (Page 122).

牛
肉
炒
鮮
菇
Beef Tenderloin and Mushrooms

1 lb. beef tenderloin
1 cup prepared dried
   mushrooms (Page 19)
1/2 t. grated garlic
2 t. cornstarch

5 T. oil
1 T. wine
3 T. soy sauce
1/2 t. sugar

Cut beef and mushrooms into strips. Sprinkle beef with grated garlic and corn-starch, heat oil and sauté over high heat until color changes. Add mushrooms and continue cooking until tender. Add wine, soy sauce and sugar and serve hot.   SERVES 4

葱
炒
牛
肉
Sautéed Beef with Leek

3/4 lb. beef
2 t. soy sauce
2 t. cornstarch
1 clove garlic

2 leeks
4 T. oil
3 T. soy sauce
1/2 t. sugar

Cut beef into strips and sprinkle with soy sauce and cornstarch. Crush garlic and cut leeks into 2″ lengths. Heat oil and sauté garlic over high heat until brown. Add beef and sauté until color changes. Add leek, soy sauce and sugar, stirring constantly. Serve hot.   SERVES 2

◄Beggar's Chicken and Chicken Puffs (Page 70): Beggar's Chicken is wrapped in lotus leaves, covered with clay and baked in an oven. This unusual cooking method is said to have originated with a starving beggar who stole a chicken but had no utensils with which to prepare his meal. He covered the bird with clay and placed it in a bonfire. The result, to his surprise and our good fortune, was delicious.

醬爆牛肉絲 Sautéed Beef with Bean Paste

3/4 lb. beef
1 leek
1 egg white
2 t. wine
2 t. cornstarch
4 T. oil
3 T. bean paste
2 T. sesame oil
6 T. water

Shred beef and leek. Soak shredded leek in water and drain. Mix beef with egg white, wine and cornstarch. Heat oil and sauté over high heat until tender. Mix bean paste, sesame oil and water together and add to beef, mixing well. Arrange on plate with shredded leek on top and serve hot.   SERVES 4

宮保羊肉 Sliced Mutton with Peppers

1/4 lb. mutton
4 T. oil
1/2 t. grated garlic
1 T. chopped red pepper
3 T. chopped leek or onion
1 cup bite-size green pepper wedges
2 cups bite-size cabbage wedges
3 T. soy sauce
1/2 t. sugar
dash of pepper

Place mutton in ample water, bring to a boil and simmer for 30 minutes or until tender. Remove mutton, cool and slice thinly. Heat oil and sauté mutton, garlic, red pepper and leek over high heat until mutton is lightly browned. Add green pepper and cabbage and stir a few minutes, adding remaining ingredients. Serve hot.   SERVES 2-4

Note: A few drops of tabasco may be substituted for red pepper.

80

炸
羊
肉 **Deep-Fried Mutton**

1 1/2 lbs. mutton
dash of salt
dash of pepper
dash of wine
2 egg whites
4 T. cornstarch
deep-frying oil
6 leeks
salt mixture (Page 25)
tomato catsup

Slice mutton 1/8″ thick and sprinkle with salt, pepper and wine. Beat egg whites with cornstarch and coat mutton with this batter, stacking slices in 3 or 4 layers. Heat oil to 335°F. and deep fry stacked mutton until crisp. Drain on absorbent paper and cut into strips. Cut leeks into 2″ lengths and arrange with mutton on serving platter. Serve hot with salt mixture and tomato catsup.　　SERVES 4-6

拌
腰
花 **Chilled Pork Kidney with Carrot**

color—page 77

2 pork kidneys
5 T. chopped leek
1 t. grated ginger
1 T. wine
18 crosswise slices carrot
1/2 t. salt
1/2 t. sugar

SAUCE:
1 t. black pepper
1 t. vinegar
2 T. soy sauce
1/2 t. sugar
1 T. wine

Cut kidneys in half lengthwise and remove white muscle. Soak in water for at least 15 minutes. Score each kidney on one side in a fine crisscross pattern, cut into bite-size pieces, and wash. Drop leek, ginger and wine in boiling water, add kidneys and stir briskly. When kidneys change color, remove from heat and drain. Allow to cool and refrigerate. Make slits along edges of carrot slices, sprinkle with salt and sugar and let stand 5 hours. Arrange kidneys and carrot slices on serving plate and serve cold with sauce as appetizer.　　SERVES 4

紅
燒
肚
子 **Braised Pork Tripe**

1 pork tripe (about 1 lb.)
1 T. salt
2 T. vinegar
1 t. black peppercorns*
1 t. star aniseeds*
  *in small cloth bag
1 T. vinegar
1 T. soy sauce
1 T. salt
4 cups wine

Turn tripe inside out and rub well with salt and vinegar. Trim yellow parts and wash well in hot water to remove odor. Bring a potful of water to a boil, add tripe and remaining ingredients and cook for 2 hours. Remove and cut into 1/2″ × 1 1/2″ strips. Serve cold with a dip of vinegar and soy sauce mixed to taste.

SERVES 2-4

酥
肉 **Braised Pork with Radish**

3/4 lb. pork
1 lb. radish
1 egg
4 T. flour

1 1/2 t. salt
deep-frying oil
2 T. soy sauce
1 T. wine

Cut pork and radish into bite-size pieces. Beat egg with flour and 1/2 t. salt to make batter. Heat oil to 335°F., dip pork in batter and deep fry until brown. Put radish, soy sauce, wine and 1 t. salt in casserole with pork on top, and add hot water to cover. Cover, bring to a boil, lower heat and continue cooking for 1 1/2 hours. Serve hot.

SERVES 4

溜
黃
菜 **Peking-Style Eggs**

6 egg yolks
1 cup broth or water
2 T. chopped ham
3/4 t. salt

82

1 T. wine
1 T. cornstarch
5 T. oil
1 T. finely chopped ham
1 T. finely chopped parsley

Beat egg yolks and mix with broth, ham, salt, wine and cornstarch. Heat oil and scramble egg mixture over high heat until fluffy. Remove to serving bowl, sprinkle with ham and parsley and serve hot. SERVES 4

菠菜炒蛋 Scrambled Eggs with Spinach

1/4 lb. spinach
3 eggs
6 T. oil
1 t. salt
dash of monosodium glutamate

Wash spinach and halve crosswise. Beat eggs lightly, heat 3 T. oil, scramble eggs and remove to plate. Heat another 3 T. oil and sauté spinach over high heat until color changes. Add scrambled eggs, salt and monosodium glutamate, stir and serve hot. SERVES 2

栗子白菜 Chinese Cabbage with Chestnuts

1 lb. Chinese cabbage
2 T. chicken fat
1 cup soup stock
1 t. salt
1/4 t. monosodium glutamate
1 T. cornstarch
3 T. water
8 canned chestnuts

Section cabbage, boil until tender and drain. Heat chicken fat and sauté cabbage. Add soup stock, salt and monosodium glutamate and bring to a boil. Mix cornstarch with water and add to thicken, stirring constantly. Arrange on serving plate, garnish with chestnuts and serve hot. SERVES 4

辣汁白菜 Tangy Chinese Cabbage

1 lb. Chinese cabbage
1 T. salt
1/2 cup water
1 T. sesame oil
1/4 cup shredded ginger
1/4 cup shredded carrot
2 red peppers
1 T. sugar
2 T. vinegar
1/2 t. salt

Slice cabbage, sprinkle with salt and water and let stand overnight. Squeeze water from cabbage and arrange on serving plate. Heat sesame oil and sauté ginger, carrot and red pepper until coated with oil. Add remaining ingredients and bring to a boil. Pour over cabbage, let stand 10 minutes or more and serve.

SERVES 4

Note: A few drops of tabasco may be substituted for red pepper.

燴菜花 Braised Cauliflower

12 oz. cauliflower
6 oz. carrot
3 T. oil
1 t. salt
1/2 t. sugar
dash of pepper
1 1/2 cups soup stock
1 1/2 t. cornstarch
1 T. water

Separate cauliflower into flowerets, parboil in salted water and drain. Slice carrot crosswise. Heat oil and sauté cauliflower and carrot over high heat, adding salt, sugar and pepper. Add soup stock and bring to a boil. Mix cornstarch with water and add to thicken. Serve hot.

SERVES 4

84

紅烧豆腐 Bean Curd with Shrimp and Chicken

1 loaf bean curd
1 T. cornstarch
5 T. oil
1/4 lb. shrimp
1/4 t. salt
1 t. wine
1/2 t. cornstarch
1/2 lb. chicken
3 prepared dried mushrooms (Page 19)
1/4 lb. bamboo shoots
5 hard-boiled quail eggs
2 cups soup stock
2 T. soy sauce
2 T. wine
1/2 t. salt

dash of black pepper
1 t. sesame oil
1 t. cornstarch
1 T. water

Drain bean curd, cut into bite-size pieces and sprinkle with cornstarch. Heat 3 T. oil and fry both sides of bean curd over medium heat until slightly brown. Set aside. Shell and devein shrimps and sprinkle with salt, wine and cornstarch. Parboil chicken and cut chicken, mushrooms and bamboo shoots into bite-size pieces. Shell hard-boiled quail eggs. Heat 2 T. oil and sauté shrimps, chicken, mushrooms and bamboo shoots over high heat until shrimps change color. Add soup stock, soy sauce, wine, salt and pepper, cover and continue cooking over medium heat until liquid is absorbed. Before removing from heat, add sesame oil and quail eggs. Mix cornstarch with water and add to thicken.   SERVES 4

拌波菜 Spinach Salad

1 lb. spinach
1 t. salt
2 slices boiled or baked ham
2 T. sesame oil

2 T. soy sauce
1 t. salt
1/2 t. sugar

Wash spinach and boil with salt for 3 minutes. Rinse in cold water, drain and chop coarsely. Place in serving bowl and chill. Chop ham and use to garnish spinach. Mix remaining ingredients together for dressing, pour over salad and toss before serving.   SERVES 4

燴 Cream Soup with Cabbage
油
白 *1/3 lb. Chinese cabbage*   *dash of monosodium glutamate*
菜 *3 cups soup stock*   *1 T. cornstarch*
湯 *1 cup milk*   *2 T. water*
  1 t. salt

Cut cabbage into bite-size pieces. Bring soup stock to a boil, add cabbage and bring to a second boil. Add milk, salt and monosodium glutamate. Mix cornstarch with water and add to thicken. Serve hot.   SERVES 4

Note: Head cabbage may be substituted.

WINTER

Cold Meat Combination
Chicken Wings and Soy Beans
Empress Chicken
Peking Duck
Peking Duck with Chinese Pancakes
Peking Duck with Pineapple
Braised Wild Duck
Steamed Fish with Chicken and Ham
Braised Shark's Fin
Sautéed Lobster with Broccoli
Crab Meat Rolls
Stuffed Clams
Fried Oysters
Braised Crab Meat and Bean Curd
Shredded Beef with Chili Peppers
Sliced Beef with Spinach
Braised Beef with Lotus Root
Spicy Steamed Beef
Braised Beef Tongue
Spicy Braised Mutton
Soy-Sauce Pork
Braised Soy-Sauce Pork
Deep-Fried Pork
Spareribs with Kumquats and Brussel Sprouts
Steamed Oysters and Egg
Steamed-Fish Omelet
Shrimp with Scrambled Egg
Sautéed Cabbage and Button Mushrooms
Sweet Kumquats
Duck Bone Soup
Hou Kuo Pot

冷
拼
盤 **Cold Meat Combination**

color—page 97

3 egg yolks
dash of salt
dash of monosodium glutamate
1 cucumber
6 canned asparagus spears
1 tomato
6 slices ham
1 braised mushroom (Page 31)
16 slices roast beef

16 slices roast pork
16 slices braised tongue (Page 101)
1 cup shredded jellyfish (Page 18)
SAUCE:
  2 T. soy sauce
  4 T. soup stock
  1 t. sesame oil

Mix egg yolks with salt and monosodium glutamate, pour into greased mold and steam over low heat for 15 minutes. Remove from steamer and cool. Cut cucumber and asparagus into 2 1/2″ lengths and slice lengthwise. Slice tomato vertically, quarter all but 2 of the ham slices, and slice braised mushroom. Remove egg from mold and slice. Arrange ingredients on a large serving plate as shown in the color photograph, making two rose shapes with the mushroom and remaining ham slices and placing jellyfish in the center. Mix sauce ingredients together and serve in separate bowl alongside cold meat plate.

Note: Soy-Sauce Beef (Page 35) and Soy-Sauce Pork (Page 102) may be substituted for roast beef and roast pork.

鶏
翅
燉 **Chicken Wings and Soy Beans**
黃
豆 *1 cup soy beans*
1 lb. chicken wings
3 T. oil
1/2 cup coarsely chopped leek
5 slices ginger
6 T. soy sauce
1 T. sugar
1 T. wine

Soak soy beans in water overnight. Wash chicken wings in hot water. Heat oil and sauté leek and ginger over high heat for 1 minute. Add chicken wings and soy beans and stir. Add soy sauce, sugar, wine and enough water to cover. Cover and simmer for 1 1/2 hours.

SERVES 4

貴妃鶏 Empress Chicken

6 spring-chicken legs
6 spring-chicken wings
2 leeks
5 prepared dried mushrooms (Page 19)
1 cup small bamboo shoots
4 T. oil
4 slices ginger
4 T. soy sauce
2 T. wine
2 cups soup stock
1 T. sugar
dash of monosodium glutamate
2 t. cornstarch
2 T. water

Wash chicken in lukewarm water. Cut leek into 2″ lengths, slice mushrooms, and cut bamboo shoots into 2″ long strips. Heat oil and sauté leek and ginger over high heat for a few minutes. Add chicken, mushrooms and bamboo shoots and continue sautéing until chicken changes color. Add soy sauce, wine and soup stock, cover and bring to a boil. Lower heat and simmer for 20 minutes. Add sugar and continue cooking 1 hour more. Before removing from heat, add monosodium glutamate, mix cornstarch with water and add to thicken, stirring constantly. Serve hot. SERVES 4

烤鴨子 Peking Duck

1 whole duck
2 T. ground black peppercorn
2 T. salt
2 T. wine
2 leeks

5 slices ginger
2 T. sesame oil
2 T. honey or plain syrup
deep-frying oil

Clean duck, wash well and dry inside and out with a cloth. Rub well with black peppercorn, salt and wine. Cut leeks into 2″ lengths and place leek and ginger in cavity of duck. Bake in slow oven until slightly brown (about 1 hour). Remove from oven and, while still hot, brush entire surface of duck first with sesame oil and then with honey. Tie legs with string and hang up to dry overnight in a well-ventilated place. Heat oil to 320°F. and deep fry until crisp, pouring hot oil over unsubmerged parts of duck. Drain.

Note: Peking duck may be served whole or may be cut into bite-size pieces, or you may choose to use the duck for Peking Duck with Chinese Pancakes, Peking Duck with Pineapple, and Duck Bone Soup.

北京烤鴨 Peking Duck with Chinese Pancakes

color—page 98

skin from 1 Peking duck (Page 90)
6 leeks
2 cucumbers
2 carrots
parsley
12 Chinese pancakes (Page 110)

BEAN PASTE MIXTURE:
2 T. oil
2 oz. bean paste
2 T. sugar
1/2 T. soy sauce

Cut duck skin into bite-size pieces. Cut leeks into 2″ lengths, shred both ends of each piece, soak in water for 10 minutes and drain. Peel cucumber, halve crosswise and quarter each half. Cut carrots into sticks. To make bean paste mixture, heat oil, add remaining ingredients and heat over a low fire. Transfer to a serving bowl. Arrange duck skin, leek and parsley on a serving platter and serve along with cucumber, carrot, pancakes and bean paste mixture.

Note: This dish is eaten by spreading each pancake with bean paste mixture and filling with pieces of duck skin and a stick each of carrot, cucumber and leek. The pancakes are then rolled and eaten with the fingers.

拌鴨肉 Peking Duck with Pineapple

color—page 98

meat from 1 whole Peking Duck
  (Page 90)
2 slices canned pineapple
1 cucumber
bean paste mixture (Page 91)

Cut duck meat into bite-size pieces and quarter pineapple. Rub cucumber with salt, wash, halve lengthwise, score and cut into bite-size pieces. Arrange duck, pineapple and cucumber on serving plate and serve with bean paste mixture.

SERVES 4

Variation: Substitute soy sauce for bean paste mixture.

紅燒全鴨 Braised Wild Duck

1 wild duck	2 T. oil
3 leeks	1/2 cup soy sauce
5 mushrooms	1 T. sugar
10 slices ginger	1 T. cornstarch
2 T. wine	2-3 T. water

Clean duck well. Cut leeks into 2″ lengths. Remove stems from mushrooms and slice. Place 2/3 of leek and 1/2 of ginger in a potful of water with wine and bring to a boil. Add duck, cover and cook for 30 minutes. Discard water and wash duck well in cold water. Cut back of duck lengthwise and open. Heat oil and sauté remaining leek and ginger over high heat until brown. Add duck and sauté until brown. Remove to deep pot, add soy sauce, sugar and enough water to cover and sprinkle with mushrooms. Bring to a boil and continue cooking 1 hour. Remove duck to serving platter. Mix cornstarch with water and add to leftover liquid to thicken. Pour this sauce over duck and serve hot.

SERVES 4

清
蒸
魚 **Steamed Fish with Chicken and Ham**

1 whole white-meat fish (about 1 1/2 lbs.)
5 slices ham
5 slices chicken fillet
4 slices mushroom
1 T. wine
1 t. salt
1 t. ginger juice
1 cup soup stock

Clean and scale fish, cut ham and chicken into 2″ × 3″ rectangles, and cut mushroom diagonally to similar dimensions. Make three slashes on each side of fish, place on plate and arrange slices of chicken, ham and mushroom on top as shown in photograph. Sprinkle with wine, salt, ginger juice and soup stock and steam over high heat for 20 minutes. Serve hot. SERVES 4

Note: Fish may be served with a dip of soy sauce and vinegar mixed to taste.

燴
蟹
粉 **Braised Shark's Fin**
魚
翅 1/4 lb. refined shark's fin

1 leek
5 slices ginger
1 can crab meat (about 3/8 lb.)
3 cups soup stock
1/2 cup shredded ham
3 T. soy sauce
1 t. sugar
2 T. wine   2 T. cornstarch
1 t. salt   4 T. water

Prepare shark's fin (Page 19). Boil shark's fin with leek and ginger until tender. Rinse well in cold water and drain. Remove filaments of crab meat and separate into flakes. Bring soup stock to a boil and add shark's fin, crab meat and ham. Continue cooking 30 minutes. Add soy sauce, sugar, wine and salt. Mix cornstarch with water and add to thicken, stirring constantly. Serve hot. SERVES 4

炒龍蝦 Sautéed Lobster with Broccoli

color—page 97

1 lobster (about 3 lbs.)
1 t. white wine or sherry
1/2 egg white
1 t. cornstarch
1 cup broccoli flowerets
3 T. oil
1 T. white wine or sherry

1/2 t. sugar
1/2 t. salt
2 T. cornstarch
1/2 cup water
deep-frying oil
1 oz. transparent vermicelli

Wash lobster in cold water, bind with string to prevent curling and steam over high heat for 20 minutes. Remove meat from shell, dice and marinate in wine, egg white and cornstarch. Parboil broccoli in salted water and soak in cold water. Heat oil and sauté lobster and broccoli for 1 minute, adding wine, sugar and salt. Mix cornstarch with water and add to thicken, stirring constantly. Heat oil to 330°F. and deep fry vermicelli. Place lobster shell on serving platter, surround with vermicelli and fill shell with lobster meat and broccoli. SERVES 4

炸蟹卷 Crab Meat Rolls

3 oz. canned crab meat
1 oz. celery
3 T. oil
1/2 t. salt
1 t. wine
dash of monosodium glutamate
30-40 3" square steamed dumpling
   wrappings (Page 112)
deep-frying oil

Remove filaments from crab and separate into flakes. Shred celery, heat oil and sauté crab meat and celery over high heat until tender. Add salt, wine and monosodium glutamate and stir. Place 1/2 t. crab meat mixture on each wrapping and fold envelope-style as illustrated. Dampen edges with water and seal. Heat oil to 340°F. and deep fry until golden. Serve as hors d'oeuvre. SERVES 6-8

蒸蛤蜊塞肉 Stuffed Clams

8 clams
1/4 lb. ground pork
1 T. wine
1/2 T. soy sauce
1 T. chopped leek

1/4 t. ginger juice
1/2 t. salt
1/4 t. sugar
2 T. cornstarch
1/2 beaten egg

Soak clams in salted water to remove sand and parboil until shells open. Mix remaining ingredients together and divide into 8 portions. Stuff one portion in each empty half-shell. Arrange all 16 half-shells on a platter and steam over high heat for 15 minutes. Serve hot.   SERVES 4

炸蛔蝗 Fried Oysters

1 lb. oysters
1 T. wine
1/2 t. salt
1 egg white
1/2 cup flour
1 t. baking powder
4 T. water
deep-frying oil

Sprinkle oysters with salt, wash, parboil and drain. Sprinkle with wine and salt. Beat egg white with flour, baking powder and water to make batter. Heat oil to 340°F., dip oysters in batter and deep fry until crisp. Serve hot.   SERVES 4

蟹粉豆腐 Braised Crab Meat and Bean Curd

1/2 lb. canned crab meat
2 loaves bean curd
4 T. oil
2 T. coarsely chopped leek
1 t. grated ginger
1 T. wine

1 T. soy sauce
1 t. sugar
1 t. salt
2 t. cornstarch
2 t. water

Remove filaments from crab meat and cut bean curd into 1″ cubes. Heat oil and sauté leek and ginger over high heat until well coated with oil. Add crab meat and mix well. Add bean curd, wine, soy sauce, sugar and salt and continue cooking 6 minutes, moving the pan gently. Mix cornstarch with water and add to thicken. Serve hot.   SERVES 4

乾
炒
牛
肉
糸
Shredded Beef with Chili Peppers

1 lb. beef loin
2 T. wine
2 T. soy sauce
6 T. oil
1 cup shredded celery
3 chili peppers
1 t. grated garlic
1/2 t. salt
1/2 t. sugar

Shred beef and marinate in wine and soy sauce for 10 minutes. Heat 3 T. oil and sauté celery over high heat until coated with oil. Remove to plate. Seed and shred chili peppers, heat another 3 T. oil and sauté beef, peppers and garlic over high heat. When the beef changes color, add salt, sugar and celery. Serve hot.   SERVES 4

Since the Ming dynasty (1368-1644) it has been customary to make meat dumplings in the shape of the coins of that time. These are eaten at New Year in the hope that the coming year will be a prosperous one for the family. *Clockwise from the top:* Sautéed Lobster with Broccoli (Page 94), Hou Kuo Pot (Page 106), Cold Meat Combination (Page 89), and Meat Dumplings (Page 115).

96

炒
辣
牛
肉
片

Sliced Beef with Spinach

1/2 lb. beef
8 T. oil
1 t. vinegar
1 T. soy sauce
1 1/2 t. sugar
12 oz. spinach or other leafy greens
1 t. salt
dash of monosodium glutamate

MARINADE:

1 T. wine
1/2 t. salt
dash of black pepper
1 egg white
1 T. cornstarch
1/2 t. grated garlic
1 T. chopped leek
1 t. grated ginger
1 t. powdered chili pepper

Slice beef thinly and cut into bite-size pieces. Mix marinade ingredients and marinate beef for 15 minutes. Heat 5 T. oil and sauté beef over high heat until color changes. Add vinegar, soy sauce and 1 t. sugar, stir well and remove to serving dish. Wash spinach and cut into 3″ lengths. Heat 3 T. oil and sauté spinach over high heat until tender. Add salt, monosodium glutamate and 1/2 t. sugar and serve with beef.   SERVES 2

◀New Year festivities in China begin with the Kitchen Festival on December 23 (on the following day in the south) and last until the Lantern Festival on January 15. According to ancient legend, the kitchen god returns to heaven on December 23 each year to report on the household where he has been staying. He receives instructions about the family's fortune for the forthcoming year and returns to his post in the household kitchen on New Year's Eve. The family purchases a new image of the god and places it on an altar in preparation for his return—hopefully with tidings of good fortune for the New Year. Peking Duck is one of the most famous Peking-style dishes. *From top to bottom:* Peking Duck with Pineapple (Page 92), Peking Duck with Chinese Pancakes (Page 91), and Duck Bone Soup (Page 106).

炒
藕
片
Braised Beef with Lotus Root

1/2 lb. sliced beef
1/2 lb. lotus root
1 t. salt
1 t. vinegar
2 cups water
5 T. oil
1 T. wine
2 T. soy sauce
1/4 t. salt
1 t. sugar

Cut beef into bite-size pieces. Peel lotus root and slice crosswise. Mix salt, vinegar and water together, soak lotus root in mixture for 10 minutes and drain. Heat 3 T. oil and sauté beef over high heat until color changes. Set aside. Heat 2 T. oil and sauté lotus until well coated with oil. Add beef and remaining ingredients and continue cooking 5 minutes. SERVES 4

蒸
米
粉
牛
肉
Spicy Steamed Beef

1 lb. beef
1 T. wine
4 T. soy sauce
1 t. salt
1 t. ginger juice
1/2 cup chopped leek
1 t. red pepper powder
1 t. vinegar
1 cup rice powder or bread crumbs
1 cup soup stock
1/2 lb. cabbage
1/4 leek

Slice beef and cut into bite-size pieces. Mix well with all but the last two ingredients. Cut cabbage into bite-size pieces and spread evenly in steamer rack. Place mixed ingredients over cabbage and steam over high heat for 1 hour. Shred leek, sprinkle over top and serve hot. SERVES 4

紅燒牛舌 Braised Beef Tongue

1 fresh beef tongue (about 2 lbs.)
1 leek or onion
6 slices ginger
4 T. soy sauce

1 t. sugar
3 T. wine
1 T. vinegar

Wash tongue and place in a pot with leek and ginger and enough water to cover. Bring to a boil, lower heat and simmer for 30 minutes. Remove tongue and let cool. Starting from the thicker end, remove skin with a knife. Cut tongue into bite-size pieces, add remaining ingredients and just enough water to cover, simmer until tender (about 1 hour) and serve hot. SERVES 4

燉羊肉 Spicy Braised Mutton

2 lbs. mutton
2 leeks
1/2 clove garlic
4 T. black peppercorns
1 T. star aniseeds
12 slices ginger
1/2 cup soy sauce
1/2 cup wine
2 T. sugar
dash of monosodium glutamate
12   3/4" thick rounds of carrot
12   3/4" thick rounds of radish

1 T. cornstarch
1/2 cup soup stock

Slice mutton 1/2" thick and drop in a potful of boiling water. Bring to a boil again and discard water. Repeat twice more. Cut leeks into 2" lengths, crush garlic, and place peppercorns and aniseeds in a small cloth bag to be discarded after use. Place mutton, leek, garlic, bagged spices, ginger, soy sauce, wine, sugar and monosodium glutamate in a pot with enough water to cover. Bring to a boil, lower heat, cover and simmer until mutton is tender (about 2 hours). Trim cut edges of vegetables slightly, making the form more oval, and boil. Arrange mutton on serving plate and surround with carrot and radish rounds. Mix cornstarch with soup stock and heat until thick, stirring constantly. Pour this sauce over vegetables and serve hot. SERVES 8

東
坡
肉 **Soy-Sauce Pork**

1/2 leek
12 oz. pork or fresh bacon
4 slices ginger
1 1/2 T. wine
2 1/2 T. soy sauce
1 T. oil
1 t. sugar
dash of monosodium glutamate
2 ground star aniseeds
1 t. cornstarch

Cut leek into 2″ lengths and place in a bowl with pork and ginger. Sprinkle with 1 T. wine and steam over high heat for 1 hour, or cook in pressure cooker until tender. Soak fat side of pork in 1 T. soy sauce for 5 minutes to color. Heat oil and sauté pork, leek and ginger over medium heat until golden brown. Slice pork, place in bowl with fat side down and sprinkle with sugar, monosodium glutamate, aniseed, 1 1/2 T. soy sauce and 1/2 T. wine. Steam over medium heat for 30‑40 minutes. Place 1/4 cup liquid from steamed pork in sauce‑pan with cornstarch and heat until it thickens, stirring constantly. Arrange pork with fat side down on plate and pour cornstarch‑thickened sauce over it. Serve hot.   SERVES 4

醬
肉 **Braised Soy-Sauce Pork**

1 leek   1/4 cup wine
1/2 cup soy sauce   1 cup water
5 slices ginger   1 lb. pork loin

Cut leek into 2″ lengths and place in a heavy pan with soy sauce, ginger, wine and water. Bring to a boil, add pork, cover and cook over high heat until it comes to a second boil. Lower heat and simmer for about an hour, turning pork occasionally. Remove from heat and allow pork to cool in liquid. Slice and arrange on serving platter, pouring some of the liquid over pork. Serve cold as an appetizer.   SERVES 6

Note: The leftover liquid may be saved and used again when you next prepare this dish.

軟炸里脊 Deep-Fried Pork

1 lb. pork fillet
2 T. soy sauce
2 t. wine
1 egg white
3 T. flour
1 t. baking powder
3 T. water
deep-frying oil
salt mixture (Page 25)

Cut pork into 20 strips and marinate in soy sauce and wine for 5 minutes. Beat egg white and mix with flour, baking powder and water to make batter. Heat oil to 340°F., dip pork in batter, and deep fry until slightly brown. Serve hot with salt mixture.

SERVES 4

糖醋排骨金橘 Spareribs with Kumquats and Brussel Sprouts

2 lbs. spareribs
2 T. wine
6 T. soy sauce
2 T. flour
2 T. cornstarch
deep-frying oil
20 kumquats
15 brussel sprouts
5 T. oil
6 T. sugar
2 T. vinegar

4 T. tomato catsup
1/2 cup water

Cut spareribs into bite-size pieces and mix well with 1 T. wine, 2 T. soy sauce, flour and 1 T. cornstarch. Heat oil to 335°F. and deep fry until crisp. Crush and seed kumquats and parboil brussel sprouts. Heat oil and sauté kumquats and brussel sprouts over high heat for 3 minutes. Add sugar, vinegar, tomato catsup, 4 T. soy sauce and 1 T. wine and bring to a boil. Mix 1 T. cornstarch with water and add to thicken, stirring constantly. Add spareribs, stir and serve hot.

SERVES 8

蒸 Steamed Oysters and Egg
蚵
蝗　4 eggs
蛋　2 cups soup stock
羹　1 t. salt
　　8 oysters
　　dash of soy sauce
　　dash of sesame oil

Beat eggs lightly and mix with soup stock and 1/2 t. salt. Pour into deep dish and steam over low heat until eggs are partially set (about 10 minutes). Sprinkle oysters with 1/2 t. salt, wash and drain. Arrange over egg and continue steaming 5 more minutes. Sprinkle with soy sauce and sesame oil and serve hot.   SERVES 4

煎 Steamed-Fish Omelet
魚
片　1/2 lb. white-meat fish　　　4 eggs
　　1 T. wine　　　　　　　　　1/2 t. sugar
　　3 slices ginger　　　　　　　dash of monosodium glutamate
　　1 1/3 t. salt　　　　　　　　4 T. oil
　　1 leek

Marinate fish in bowl with wine, ginger, 1/3 t. salt and 2″ lengths of leek for 15 minutes. Place bowl in steamer and steam 10 minutes. Remove fish and flake. Beat eggs with sugar, monosodium glutamate, and 1 t. salt, and mix with flaked fish. Heat oil, pour in egg-fish mixture, fry on both sides over low heat until slightly brown and serve hot.   SERVES 2

蝦 Shrimp with Scrambled Egg
仁
炒　1/2 lb. shrimp
蛋　1 t. wine
　　1/2 t. ginger juice
　　1/2 t. cornstarch
　　2 t. salt
　　7 T. oil
　　6 eggs
　　dash of monosodium glutamate

104

Shell and devein shrimps and marinate in wine, ginger juice, cornstarch and 1 t. salt for 5 minutes. Heat 2 T. oil and sauté shrimps over high heat until color changes. Remove to plate and cool. Beat eggs lightly with monosodium glutamate and 1 t. salt and mix with shrimps. Heat 5 T. oil, pour in egg-shrimp mixture and stir with a large, sweeping motion. Serve hot.　　　SERVES 4

炒
捲
心
菜

Sautéed Cabbage and Button Mushrooms

1 lb. cabbage
1/2 cup canned button mushrooms
1 clove garlic
3 T. oil
1/2 t. soy sauce
1/2 t. sugar

Cut cabbage into bite-size pieces, slice mushrooms vertically, and crush garlic. Heat oil and sauté garlic over high heat until color changes. Remove. Add cabbage and sauté over high heat for 1-2 minutes. Add mushrooms and remaining ingredients, mix well and serve hot.　　　SERVES 4

密
餞
金
橘

Sweet Kumquats

1 1/2 lbs. kumquats
1 cup crystal sugar
2 cups water

Wash kumquats and crush with knife or jar to remove seeds. Put crystal sugar and water in a pan and heat until sugar melts. Add kumquats, cover and simmer until liquid becomes thick and translucent (about 40 minutes). Serve hot or cold.

Note: These kumquats will keep for a long time in sterilized and tightly covered jars. Use in small quantities as appetizers or garnishes (also see Page 57).

鴨
骨
湯 **Duck Bone Soup**

color—page 98

bones from 1 Peking duck (with a
   little meat left on them)
1 lb. Chinese cabbage
8 cups water

2 t. salt
dash of monosodium glutamate
dash of pepper

Cut duck bones into 1"–2" lengths and cut Chinese cabbage coarsely. Bring water to a boil, add bones and cabbage and boil for 20 minutes. When meat separates easily from bones, add salt, pepper and monosodium glutamate. Serve hot.
                                                   SERVES 4

火
鍋
子 **Hou Kuo Pot**

color—page 97

1 egg
4 T. cornstarch
1/4 t. salt
deep-frying oil
1/2 lb. pork fillet
1/2 lb. Chinese cabbage
1/4 lb. transparent vermicelli
1/8 lb. prepared dried mushrooms (Page 19)
1/2 lb. bamboo shoots

1/2 lb. chicken fillet
1/4 lb. canned abalone
1/2 lb. sliced ham
3 T. canned green peas
5 cups (or more) hot soup stock
1 T. salt
2 T. wine

Beat egg with cornstarch and salt. Heat oil to 335°F., dip pork in egg mixture, deep fry until crisp and slice. Cut Chinese cabbage into bite-size pieces. Soak vermicelli in hot water and cut into 2" lengths. Slice mushrooms, bamboo shoots, chicken and abalone, and cut ham slices in half. Put cabbage and vermicelli in pot, arrange pork, mushrooms, bamboo shoots, chicken, abalone, ham and green peas on top, and add hot soup stock until pot is 3/4 full. Place burning charcoal in the chamber under the chimney, cover with lid, and add remaining ingredients.
                                                  SERVES 4–6

Note: The above quantities may be too much to cook and serve at once, and the food can be best enjoyed if you add the meats and vegetables to the pot several times rather than all at once. Add fresh ingredients as the cooked ones are eaten and allow each person to serve himself. In this way each mouthful will be fresh and hot and nothing will become over-cooked.

RICE DUMPLINGS NOODLES

Shrimp Fried Rice on Lettuce
Fish or Chicken Congee
Baked Beef Rice with Cabbage
Mandarin Pancake Rolls
Four-Color Steamed Dumplings
Meat Dumplings
Chinese Noodles
Chilled Noodles with Sauce
Fried Noodles with Assorted Meats
Chinese Bread

蛋
炒 **Shrimp Fried Rice on Lettuce**
飯 color—page 114

4 cups cooked rice	8 T. oil
8 shrimps	1 T. canned green peas
6 eggs	1 t. salt
8 large lettuce leaves	dash of pepper

Allow rice to cool. Shell and devein shrimps, beat eggs lightly, and wash and drain lettuce. Heat 6 T. oil and scramble eggs. Set aside. Add 2 T. oil to skillet and sauté shrimps over high heat until just tender. Set aside. Sauté rice over medium heat with oil left in skillet, using a wooden spoon to separate rice. Add eggs, green peas, salt and pepper and stir for 1 minute. Arrange fried rice on lettuce and garnish with shrimps. Serve hot. SERVES 4

魚 **Fish or Chicken Congee**
粥

3/4 cup rice
8-10 cups water
1/2 lb. white-meat fish or chicken
1 t. ginger juice
2 T. soy sauce
3 T. chopped leek
1 t. sesame oil
1 T. wine
1/2 cup soup stock

Wash rice, put in a large pot with water, cover tightly and bring to a boil. Lower heat and simmer 30-40 minutes. Slice fish as thinly as possible and arrange in individual bowls. Sprinkle with ginger juice. Mix remaining ingredients together well for sauce. To serve, pour rice gruel (congee) over fish and add sauce to taste. Serve hot. SERVES 4

牛
肉 **Baked Beef Rice with Cabbage**
飯

1 cup rice	1 T. wine
1/2 lb. sliced beef	3 T. soy sauce
1/4 lb. cabbage	2 cups soup stock
1/2 t. grated garlic	dash of monosodium glutamate

Wash and drain rice. Cut beef and cabbage into bite-size pieces. Marinate beef in garlic, wine and 1 T. soy sauce for 10 minutes. Mix cabbage, beef and rice and place in greased baking dish. Add soup stock, sprinkle with monosodium glutamate and 2 T. soy sauce and cover tightly. Place in a slow oven (300°F.) and bake until beef is tender and rice fluffy (about 30 minutes). Serve hot.

SERVES 2

春餅 Mandarin Pancake Rolls
color—page 113

PANCAKES

2 cups sifted all-purpose flour
2 T. sesame oil
3/4 cup boiling water (about)

Put flour and 1 T. sesame oil in a bowl and mix with chopsticks or a fork while slowly adding water. Knead well into a soft dough, form into a long sausage shape, 1 1/2" in diameter, and cut into 14 pieces. Flatten each piece lightly with the palm of your hand and roll into disks 3" in diameter. Apply a light coat of sesame oil to one side of each disk with a pastry brush, join pairs of disks in sandwiches with the oiled side in (Fig. 1), and roll into 6" disks (as thin as possible). Fry in a flat, ungreased skillet over a low heat, turning once, until both sides are slightly browned (Fig. 2). Remove from skillet and separate into two thin pancakes (Fig. 3). Line steamer with cheesecloth and steam pancakes for 10 minutes before serving. Fold into halves or quarters and cover with a cloth to keep hot until ready to serve. Serve pancakes with bean paste mixture (Page 91), shredded leek, and all or any of the following fillings.

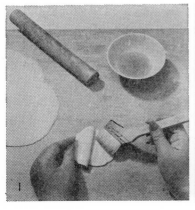

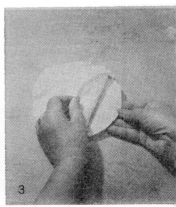

FILLINGS

SCRAMBLED EGGS

3 eggs
1 t. salt
3 T. oil

Beat eggs lightly with salt, heat oil, pour in egg mixture and cook 2 minutes, stirring constantly.

ROAST PORK

1 lb. lean pork   *6 T. soy sauce*
1 leek   *4 thin slices ginger*
1 clove garlic   *2 T. wine*

Cut pork into long strips, 2″ thick and 2″ wide. Chop leek finely and crush garlic. Mix garlic and leek with remaining ingredients for marinade and marinate pork overnight or for half a day. Heat oven to 350°F., grease rack and roast pork for 35 minutes. Turn strips once halfway through roasting time. Remove from oven, shred and serve cold.

SAUTÉED JUTS'AI WITH PORK

1 lb. juts'ai *or spring onion*   *1 t. cornstarch*
1/4 lb. pork   *5 T. oil*
2 T. soy sauce   *1/2 t. salt*
1 T. wine

Cut *juts'ai* into 2″ lengths and shred pork. Mix pork with soy sauce, wine and cornstarch. Heat oil and sauté pork until color changes. Add *juts'ai* and salt and mix well. Remove from heat before *juts'ai* loses moisture.

SAUTÉED SHRIMP

1 lb. shrimp   *3 T. oil*
1 t. cornstarch   *dash of salt*
1 t. wine

Shell and devein shrimps and sprinkle with cornstarch and wine. Heat oil and sauté over high heat until color changes. Add salt and stir well.

FRIED POTATOES

2 medium-size potatoes   *deep-frying oil*   *dash of salt*

Peel and shred potatoes, soak in water for 10 minutes, drain and dry with cheesecloth. Heat oil and deep fry until golden brown. Stir to prevent potatoes from sticking together. Sprinkle with salt while still hot.

Note: Mandarin pancakes are eaten with the fingers. Spread with bean paste mixture, fill with bits of filling and shredded leek and roll from the edge.

四喜燒売 Four-Color Steamed Dumplings

color—page 114

1/2 lb. ground pork	1 cup all-purpose flour
1/2 T. wine	1 cup cake flour
1 T. soy sauce	1 cup boiling water (about)
1/4 t. sugar	1 hard-boiled egg
1/2 T. sesame oil	1/2 cup chopped ham
1/2 cup water	1/2 cup chopped parsley
1/2 t. salt	

Mix the first seven ingredients together for filling and let stand in bowl while preparing wrappings. Sift flour and mix with boiling water, stirring briskly with chopsticks or a fork until cool enough to handle. Knead well, cover dough with damp cloth and let stand 15 minutes or more. Remove to a floured board, shape into a long sausage and cut into 12 circles. Flatten each circle with your hand and roll into a thin pancake. Separate filling into 12 portions and put one portion in the center of each wrapping. Holding the wrapping with both hands, press thumbs and forefingers together at the center of the dumpling, leaving four open corners. Separate yolk and white of hard-boiled egg and chop. Arrange egg white, egg yolk, ham, and parsley in the four open corners of each dumpling. Steam for 15 minutes and serve hot.

Mandarin Pancake Rolls (Page 110): It is customary▶ to serve this treat on the first day of spring. The fillings pictured here are, *clockwise from the top:* scrambled eggs, fried potatoes, sautéed shrimp, and roast pork, with sautéed *juts'ai* with pork in the center.

水
餃
子

Meat Dumplings

color—page 97

2 cups all-purpose flour
1 cup hot water (about)
FILLING:
    1/2 lb. Chinese cabbage or celery
    salt
    1 leek
    1/2 lb. ground pork
    1 t. grated ginger
    1/2 t. salt
    1 T. wine
    3 T. sesame oil
    dash of pepper
    dash of monosodium glutamate
soy sauce
vinegar

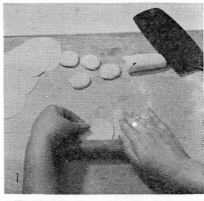

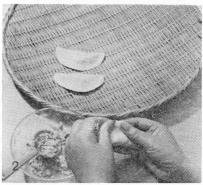

Mix flour and hot water and knead well into a soft dough. Cover with a damp cloth and let stand at least 20 minutes. Knead again and form into a long sausage 1 1/2″ in diameter. Cut into 1/3″ thick pieces. Sprinkle board with flour, flatten pieces of dough with the palm of your hand, and roll to form thin disks 4″ in diameter. Chop Chinese cabbage finely, sprinkle lightly with salt and squeeze out water with a cheesecloth. Chop leek, place cabbage and leek in a bowl with other filling ingredients and mix well. Place about 1 t. of filling in the center of each disk, fold into half-moon shapes, and seal edges with fingers (Fig. 2). Bring a deep pan of water to a boil and drop dumplings in one by one. When water comes to a boil again, add 1/2 cup of cold water. Repeat twice more, remove dumplings and serve in bowls with the water in which they were boiled, accompanied by small dishes of soy sauce and vinegar mixed to taste.

Variation: 3 T. salad oil mixed with 2 T. grated sesame seeds may be substituted for sesame oil in the filling.

◄*From top to bottom:* Chilled Noodles with Sauce (Page 117), Shrimp Fried Rice on Lettuce (Page 109), and Four-Color Steamed Dumplings (Page 112).

115

麵条 Chinese Noodles

2 eggs
dash of salt
2 cups bread flour (about)

Beat eggs lightly with salt and mix with flour. Knead well into a soft dough. Cover with a damp cloth and let stand at least 20 minutes. Knead again firmly and place on a floured board. Roll dough until about 1/8″ thick (Fig. 1). Spread flat and fold three times (Figs. 2-3). Cut across folds forming thin strips (Fig. 4). Open folds, grasp the strips by one end (Fig. 5) and sweep across a floured board several times to prevent sticking (Fig. 6). Drop noodles into a large pan of boiling water. When the water comes to a second boil, add 1 cup cold water and bring to a boil once more. Remove noodles, rinse in cold water and drain.

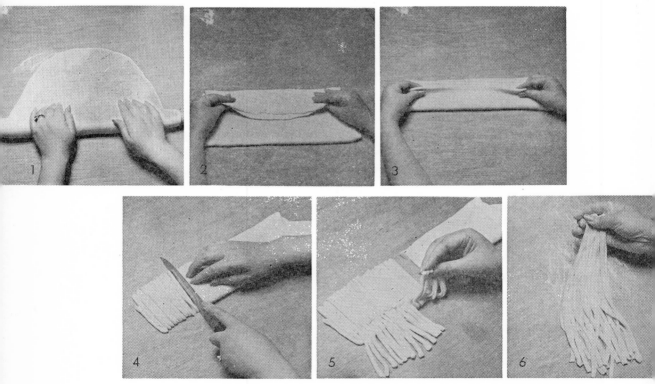

Note: Since Chinese noodles are usually made without eggs, the following recipe may be substituted for the one above (preparation is the same): 1 cup water (about), dash of salt, 2 cups bread flour.

冷拌麵 Chilled Noodles with Sauce

color—page 114

4 cups cooked noodles (Page 116)
1 T. sesame or salad oil
1 cup shredded cooked chicken
1 cup shredded cucumber
1/2 cup shredded egg sheet (Page 41)
1 T. sesame oil
1 T. chopped leek
1 T. soy sauce

1 T. wine
1 T. vinegar
1 t. tabasco or chili sauce
1/2 t. sugar
1 t. salt
dash of monosodium glutamate
1/2 cup soup stock

While still hot, mix noodles with oil to prevent sticking and place on serving plate. Allow to cool in refrigerator. Arrange chicken, cucumber and egg on top as shown in color photograph. Mix remaining ingredients for sauce and serve over noodles. Toss before eating. SERVES 4

Variation: Roasted sesame seeds may be added to the sauce.

什錦炒麵 Fried Noodles with Assorted Meats

1/4 lb. sliced pork
1 t. soy sauce
1 1/2 t. cornstarch
1/4 lb. sliced chicken
1 1/2 t. salt
4 prawns
1/2 lb. ham
5 prepared dried mushrooms (Page 19)

7 T. oil
1/2 lb. cooked noodles (Page 116)
1/2 cup sliced abalone
4 cups soup stock or water
2 T. wine
2 T. soy sauce
3 T. cornstarch
6 T. water

Sprinkle pork with soy sauce and 1 t. cornstarch, and chicken with 1/2 t. salt and 1/2 t. cornstarch. Shell prawns and slice prawns, ham and mushrooms. Heat 3 T. oil and fry noodles in one big pancake, turning once, until both sides are golden brown. Remove to a plate. Heat 4 T. oil and sauté pork, chicken, prawns, ham, mushrooms and abalone. Add soup stock, wine, soy sauce and 1 t. salt and bring to a boil. Mix cornstarch with water and add to thicken. Pour over noodles and serve hot. SERVES 2

饅 Chinese Bread
頭

2 cups cake flour
2 cups bread flour
4 t. dry yeast
2 t. sugar
1/2 t. salt
1-1 1/2 cups lukewarm water (about)
2 T. sesame oil

Sift cake and bread flour together. Dissolve yeast, sugar and salt in lukewarm water in a large bowl. Add flour, mix well and knead into a soft, smooth dough. Place dough in a bowl, cover and let stand in a warm place for 1 hour. When dough has risen, knead again to remove air bubbles. Place on a floured board and form into a long sausage 1 1/2" in diameter. Cut into 1" thick pieces, flatten each piece with the palm of your hand, and roll into "doilies" 3"-4" in diameter. Brush one side with sesame oil and fold in half (Fig. 1). Make decorative impressions on one side with a knife (Fig. 2) and use a chopstick to form leaf shapes (Fig. 3). Place in steamer, steam 15 minutes and serve hot. SERVES 4

Note: 2 t. yeast may be used instead of 4 t. if you allow 2 hours for the dough to rise. Chinese bread may be reheated either by steaming again for a short while or by warming in an oven.

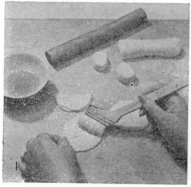

DESSERTS

Sweet Rice in Bamboo Leaves
Moon Cakes
Orange Tea
Pears in Syrup
Steamed Pine Nut Cake
Chestnut Cream Treasure
Glazed Red Dates and Strawberries
Sesame Cookies
Peach-Shaped Pastry (Chinese Birthday Cake)
Almond Bean Curd
Sweet Potato Balls
Fried Cookies

粽 **Sweet Rice in Bamboo Leaves**
子 color—page 37

5 cups glutinous rice
bamboo leaves
10 seeded dates
string
sugar

Soak rice in water overnight and drain. Roll each bamboo leaf into a cone and fill with 1 cup rice (Fig. 1). Place two dates in each cone and wrap and tie leaves tightly with string. (Figs. 2-3). Bring a large potful of water to a boil, put in bamboo-wrapped rice and boil 1-2 hours. Remove from water and cool. Unwrap leaves, slice and serve with sugar.

Note: Use two or three leaves for one wrapping if leaves are small. The amount of rice used to fill the leaves may vary with the size of the leaves, and palm or other leaves known to be safe for cooking may be substituted for bamboo.
Variation: Mix rice with salted and diced pork or ham and hard-boiled egg in place of dates and serve with salt instead of sugar for a change from the sweeter recipe above.

月餅 Moon Cakes

color—page 77

4 cups cake flour
4 oz. sugar
4 oz. lard or shortening
1/4 cup hot water
FILLING:
    2 T. finely chopped peanuts
    2 T. toasted sesame seeds
    2 T. raisins
    2 T. pine nuts
    2 T. finely chopped chestnuts
    6 T. sugar
    1 T. lard
    2 T. rice powder or toasted flour
    2 T. water
oil
1 egg yolk
1 t. sesame oil

Put flour, sugar and lard in a bowl and mix well. Add hot water and knead into dough. Place all ingredients for filling in bowl and mix well. Coat inside of mold (photo above) thinly with oil and spread a thin layer of dough (1/5″) on the bottom and sides of mold. Place 1 T. filling over dough and press. Cover with another thin layer of dough and seal. Invert on a greased baking pan, mix egg yolk with sesame oil and brush cake with mixture. Repeat for 8 cakes or until all ingredients are used. Bake in a slow oven (250°F.) for about 20 minutes.

Variation: substitute a mixture of dried fruits for the above filling.

橘子茶 Orange Tea

color—page 125

8 red dates or 1/2 cup raisins
2 1/2 cups juice from canned mandarin oranges
1 cup canned mandarin oranges
sugar

Soak dates in hot water until soft and drain. Bring juice to a boil, add dates and oranges. Add sugar to taste and serve hot or cold.

梨 羹 Pears in Syrup

2 pears
6 cups water
1 cup raisins

3/4 cup crystal sugar
3 T. cornstarch
6 T. water

Quarter pears, remove seeds and peel. Soak in salted water to prevent discoloring and slice. Bring water to a boil and add raisins and crystal sugar. Bring to a second boil, add pears and cook until it boils once more. Mix cornstarch with water and add to thicken. Serve hot.

SERVES 4

松 子 糕 Steamed Pine Nut Cake
color—page 125

2 cups cake flour
1/4 t. baking powder
5-6 eggs
1 1/2 cups sugar
3 T. pine nuts

Put flour in a bowl, steam 10 minutes, spread on paper and allow to cool. Mix with baking powder and sift. Beat eggs for 30 minutes, adding sugar gradually. Mix egg mixture with flour and baking powder. Grease an 8″ square baking pan. Cut waxed paper slightly larger than bottom of pan. Place waxed paper in pan, pour in cake batter and steam over high heat for 10 minutes. Sprinkle with pine nuts and continue steaming 10 minutes more. Remove pan and paper, cut in diamond shapes and serve hot or cold.

Variation: Substitute your favorite nuts for pine nuts.

栗
子
粉
Chestnut Cream Treasure

color—page 125

2 lbs. chestnuts
2 hard-boiled egg yolks
sugar
water
12 walnuts
12 red dates
1 cup heavy cream

Boil chestnuts until tender (about 30 minutes or, if using pressure cooker, about 15 minutes). Halve and remove meat with a small spoon. Mash and press through a sieve. Also mash and press egg yolks through a sieve. Mix chestnuts, egg yolks and 1 1/2 cups sugar together well and set aside. Shell walnuts. Soak dates in lukewarm water until tender and remove seeds. Heat 2 T. sugar and 2 T. water until sugar melts, dip walnuts and dates in one by one and set aside. To make sugar threads, place two pairs of chopsticks, one pair at either end of a long pan, leaving a space of 1 foot between. Heat 1 cup sugar and 1/2 cup water in a small saucepan until sugar melts and forms a thread when dropped from a spoon. Hold saucepan over long pan, dip into melted sugar with another pair of chopsticks and draw sugar out in threads, moving back and forth over the chopsticks on the pan with a long sweeping motion. The sugar will fall in fine strands over the chopsticks. Repeat process until all melted sugar is used. Whip heavy cream with 2 T. sugar. Arrange chestnut mixture on serving plates, garnish with glazed dates and walnuts and whipped cream, and top with sugar threads.

Upper left: Orange Tea (Page 122), *upper right:* ▶
Steamed Pine Nut Cake (Page 123), *lower left:* Chestnut Cream Treasure (Page 124), *lower right:* Glazed Red Dates and Strawberries (Page 127).

124

密餞紅棗·洋莓 Glazed Red Dates and Strawberries

color—page 125

6 red dates
2 T. oil
8 T. sugar
1 T. water
8 strawberries

Soak dates in hot water until soft (at least an hour) and seed. Heat oil over low heat, add sugar and stir. Add water to melt sugar, stirring constantly. When sugar becomes syrupy, dip strawberries and dates in one by one until well coated. Dip in cold water and allow to cool. When cool, spear with skewers and serve.

芝蔴餅 Sesame Cookies

color—page 126

1 cup sifted cake flour   1 T. water
4 T. lard   2 T. sesame seeds
1/2 cup sugar
1/2 t. salt
1 egg
1 egg yolk

Combine flour, lard, sugar, salt and egg in a bowl and knead well into a soft dough. Place on a floured board and form into a long sausage 1 1/2" in diameter. Cut into 36 pieces and flatten each with the palm of your hand. Mix egg yolk with water and brush mixture on one side of each piece of dough. Sprinkle brushed side of dough with sesame seeds and press to adhere. Place on greased cookie sheet and bake in medium oven (350°F.) for 15 minutes.

◀ *Clockwise from the top:* Fried Cookies, Sesame Cookies, Sweet-Potato Balls, Almond Bean Curd, and Peach-Shaped Pastry (Pages 127-130).

Peach-Shaped Pastry
(Chinese Birthday Cake)

color—page 126

4-6 t. dry yeast	8 cups sifted cake flour
2 t. sugar	1/2 lb. sweet bean paste
2 1/2 cups lukewarm water (about)	sesame oil
2 T. sugar	dash of red food coloring
1/2 t. salt	

Dissolve yeast with sugar in 1/2 cup lukewarm water and let stand 5 minutes. Add yeast mixture, sugar and salt to flour, mix well and knead into a soft dough, gradually adding water. Cover, put in warm place and let stand 1 1/2 hours. Place on floured board, knead again and form into long sausage 1 1/2" in diameter. Divide dough in half, set one half aside, and divide the other into 12 pieces for small pastries. Flatten each piece with your hand and roll into a small circle about 3" in diameter. Place 1/12 of bean paste in the center of each circle and wrap in the form of a peach. Make a large peach shape with 2/3 of the remaining dough, and brush the surface with sesame oil. Roll the remaining 1/3 into a large circle and wrap around the large peach-shaped dough. Dilute food coloring with a little water and redden the top of each pastry by running a knife across the bristles of a toothbrush dipped in the coloring (see photograph). Steam pastries over high heat for 20 minutes. Make a cut around 3/4 the circumference of the large pastry and lift out the inner peach shape. Put the small "peaches" in the cut shell and serve hot.

Note: Slice the large "peach" that has been removed from its shell and serve as bread with other dishes.

杏
仁
豆
腐 **Almond Bean Curd**

color—page 126

2 envelopes gelatin or 1 agar-agar
3 3/4 cups water
6 T. condensed milk
1 T. almond extract
15 canned grapes
5 strawberries
1 cup syrup from canned grapes

Dissolve gelatin in water and bring to a boil. Strain liquid through cheesecloth or sieve. Add condensed milk and almond extract and stir well. Pour into bowl, allow to set, and cool in refrigerator. Cut in diamond shapes, garnish with grapes and strawberries and pour syrup over the top.

Variation: Other fruits may be substituted for grapes and strawberries. 1 cup fresh milk may be substituted for condensed milk if you use 3 cups instead of 3 3/4 cups water and 3 T. sugar in place of almond extract.

炸
白
薯
球 **Sweet Potato Balls**

color—page 126

1 1/2 lbs. sweet potatoes
5 T. sugar
1/2 cup flour
1/4 t. salt
1 egg
deep-frying oil
1 T. powdered sugar

Wash and peel sweet potatoes and steam or boil over high heat until very soft. Mash and sieve to remove stringy fibers. Mix with sugar, flour, salt and egg and form small balls using a tablespoon (Page 54). Heat oil to 330°F. and deep fry over medium heat until slightly brown. Drain on absorbent paper and, using a sieve, sprinkle with powdered sugar (see photograph).

Note: Try this sweet with turkey at your next Christmas or Thanksgiving dinner.

129

炸
蔴
花 **Fried Cookies**

color—page 126

2 cups sifted cake flour
1/2 cup sugar
1 T. sesame seeds
1 T. lard or shortening
6 T. water (about)
deep-frying oil

Combine all ingredients except oil in a bowl and knead well into a soft dough. Place on a floured board and roll as thin as possible (1/8″ or thinner). Cut into 3/4″ × 2″ rectangles and make a lengthwise slit in the center of each. Bring one end of the strip through the slit to form a twist (see illustrations). Heat oil to 335°F. and deep fry until golden brown.

WINE, TEA AND THE TABLE

TABLE SETTING AND DINNER MENUS

Porcelain and silver tableware are important elements that enhance the atmosphere of a Chinese dinner. Silverware has been used in China since ancient times. It was not only appreciated for its glittering beauty, but the emperors and lords of ancient China used it as a means of discovering the presence of poison in the food served them—silver easily discolors when dipped in poison.

The tableware required for an individual place setting at a Chinese meal consists of rice and soup bowls, one or two varieties of dishes, small dishes for dips or condiments, chopsticks, and a porcelain spoon (Fig. 1). A wide range of attractive Western and Japanese tableware is also available today and may be substituted for Chinese tableware, so one can set a beautiful table without purchasing a collection of expensive Chinese dishes.

◀This slightly unorthodox, but delightful table setting illustrates how Western tableware can be successfully used in combination with Chinese wares. The glasses and silver are Danish; the soup bowls, place mats, flower vase, and folding screen are Chinese.

In Chinese cuisine it is customary to plan a meal which consists of a variety of dishes that differ from one another both in the kind of ingredients used and the method of preparation. For example, if the chicken dish on your menu is sautéed, the fish dish should be deep fried, and the other meat dishes steamed or served with a cornstarch-thickened sauce.

Most of the recipes in this book will serve four or six people, and if a greater quantity is required, it is always preferable to add extra dishes to your menu rather than increase the quantity of individual dishes. An informal Chinese meal usually consists of four courses: an appetizer, an assorted cold dish, a sautéed or fried dish, and a steamed or braised dish with which rice and soup are served. A formal meal usually consists of eight, ten, or twelve courses—even numbers are considered lucky—depending upon the importance of the occasion and the budget of the host. Formal dinners begin with a cold dish such as the colorfully arranged assortment of appetizers on page 89. Such dishes are especially delicious when served with wine. The usual order of courses following the appetizer is chicken, fish, shellfish, beef, pork, egg, bean curd, vegetables, soup, and, if desired, dessert. The dishes are attractively arranged on large serving platters and placed at the center of the table. The guest of honor is, of course, offered the first serving.

BASIC RULES IN PLANNING A CHINESE DINNER

1. Do not use the same ingredients repeatedly. It is preferable that each course have a different main ingredient.
2. The methods of preparation of the different courses should also be varied.
3. Select dishes that are seasoned in various ways. In other words, if you include a salty dish, also include a sweet-and-sour dish, a lightly seasoned and a heavily seasoned dish.
4. After the appetizer, the courses should proceed from the lightly seasoned to the heavily seasoned dishes.

TABLE MANNERS

Although rigid table manners are not required at Chinese meals there are a few basic rules of etiquette that are observed. The most important thing, however, is that everyone enjoys his meal.

1. The food is arranged in large serving platters in the center of the table and serving chopsticks or a serving spoon are usually provided. If they are not available, however, you may use your own chopsticks or spoon to carry the food to your plate.

2. When serving yourself from a large platter of cold appetizers, take three or four varieties of food at a time and be sure to serve yourself from the top so that you do not disturb the arrangement.

3. Since the dinner will consist of many dishes, help yourself to only a moderate amount of each course so that you will be able to taste all the courses and appreciate the meal as a whole.

4. The table is often set with a lazy susan that can be revolved so that each guest can reach the serving platters with ease and there is no need to pass the platters around the table. If, however, there is no lazy susan and dishes must be passed, hold the platter with both hands and be careful not to brush it against the other dishes on the table.

5. The food should be adequately seasoned before it is served and there should not be many additional seasonings at the table.

6. When the meal is one-pot cuisine, take ingredients to your dish before they reach your mouth (this rule also applies to all other types of dishes as well). Extra seasonings may be added if necessary, and the soup should be served separately.

7. When fried noodles are served in a large platter, take a small amount on your own dish, using serving chopsticks and a porcelain spoon. When noodles in broth are served, take the noodles and solid ingredients to your bowl with chopsticks and pour the broth over the noodles with a spoon. The broth should also be drunk with the spoon.

8. Large whole fish is served on a platter with its belly toward the guest. The head may be either on the left or the right. The hostess scores the fish with a knife and serves her guests. After the upper half of the fish is served, she removes the bones and offers more to the guests. The custom of turning the belly of the fish toward the guest has survived since ancient times when it was an assurance that there was no knife in the belly with which to assassinate him.

9. When foods with bones or shells are served, remove the bone or shell in your mouth so that you will enjoy the full flavor of the food, and return the bone or shell to the plate with your chopsticks rather than your fingers. (You may, of course, remove the bones or shells on your plate.)

10. Dumplings, buns, and pancake rolls may be eaten with the fingers.

Chinese Wines

As in many other countries, wine is indispensable at banquets and dinner parties in China. Chinese wine, like Japanese saké, is usually served warm (115°F.). Wine has a long history in China and various ancient legends tell of alcoholic beverages. Wine was first presented to Emperor Yu of the Hsiah Dynasty (2200

2. Four varieties of Chinese wine.
3. Small porcelain cups and kettle- and pitcher-like servers
in which the wine is heated to 115°F.

B.C.) by I-Ti, a member of his court. The Emperor, however, feared that alcohol would have evil effects in the future and instead of welcoming the drink and honoring I-Ti, he had him demoted.

Chinese wines are divided into two general classes, the brewed and the distilled. The former, which can be simply produced, has a longer history, whereas distilled liquor—according to ancient records—was first produced during the Yüan Dynasty in the thirteenth century.

The following are some popular wines in present-day China:

Shoahsing is a yellow-colored wine made of fermented glutinous rice and is named after the place where it is mainly produced, Shaohsing in Chekiang Province. It is aged for at least one year.

Lao Chiew is the above *Shaohsing* that has been allowed to age for a longer period of time and is served with chipped crystal sugar. It is an old custom to bury a number of jars of *Shaohsing* when a girl is born. The wine is allowed to age until her marriage, at which time the family has an ample stock of well-aged *Lao Chiew* to celebrate the occasion with its guests.

Meikuei Chiew is scented with dried wild roses and is a special favorite of women. White wines are made from *kaoliang* (sweet corn and barley) and are especially delicious with foods that have been cooked in oil. There are three varieties which differ in alcoholic content: *Yang Kuei Fei* (20%), *Pai Kan* (35%), and *Kaoliang Chiew* (50%).

Ng Ka Py is made with such herbs as tea leaves and acothopanax root and is considered the elixir of life among Chinese wines.

Mou-tai Chiew is named for Mou-tai Chen, Jen Hwai city in the northern part of Kweichow Province, where, for over two centuries, it has been fermented and distilled from the best wheat and millet and the famous Mou-tai Fountain water. It is aged in cellars for a considerably long time before it is bottled.

CHINESE TEA

According to third-century documents, tea leaves were packed in solid cakes and these were chipped and crushed, mixed with onion, ginger, orange peel, etc., boiled, and drunk as a medicinal beverage, rather than for refreshment. During the Three Dynasties period (220-280), tea drinking became popular in connection with the rise of Zen Buddhism. The cultivation of tea bushes and the drinking of tea by placing the leaves in boiling water are mentioned in the *Erh-ya*, written by Kuo P'o in the fourth century.

Tea drinking became extremely popular during the Sui and T'ang dynasties and its cultivation and preparation developed accordingly. The "Tea Classic," written by Yu-lu in 760, became the standard tea ceremony text and served to spread the practice to other parts of the world.

Tea remains the most popular drink in China and attractive tea stands are located along streets in crowded centers of Peking. Here people can sit and enjoy a cup of tea as well as buy tea to take home with them. There are numerous varieties of Chinese tea. Some well-known green teas are *Yangshen Cha, Moli Cha,* and *Lungching. Hsiangpien,* with its delightful aroma of dried orchid, narcissus, or Japanese Judas blossom, is also a popular choice. Beside the well-known Jasmine tea with its delicate floral aroma, other delicious black teas are *Lapsang Souchong, Keemun,* and *Lichee.*

The proper way to prepare tea is to place a teaspoon of tea leaves in a teacup, spread the leaves, and pour boiling water over them. The cup should be covered with its lid until the leaves settle to the bottom. Slide the lid away slightly and sip the tea through the small opening between lid and cup (Fig. 4). Tea may also be prepared in a teapot. Cookies and pastries are usually served with tea and a cup of Chinese tea is especially refreshing after a full meal since many of the dishes will have been cooked with oil. Porcelain and ceramic wares are thought best for tea cups since they can keep the tea hot for quite some time.

Glossary

Beverages
Tea (*Ch'a:* 茶)
Wine (*Chiu:* 酒)

Cooking Methods
Baking (*Ka'o:* 烤)
Braising (*Tun:* 燉)
Deep frying (*Ch'a:* 炸)
Mixing (*P'an:* 拌)
Sautéing (*Ch'ao:* 炒)
Simmering (*Hung Shao:* 紅燒)
Soup (*T'ang:* 湯)
Steaming (*Chêng:* 蒸)

Cutting Methods
Chopping (*Sung:* 鬆)
Cubing (*Ting:* 丁)
Shredding (*Ssu:* 糸)
Slicing (*P'ien:* 片)

Fish and Crustaceans
Abalone (*Pao yü:* 鮑魚)
Bêche-de-mer (*Hai shen:* 海參)
Clam (*Ko li:* 蛤蜊)
Crab (*Hsieh:* 蟹)
Jellyfish (*Hai chê:* 海蜇)
Lobster (*Lung hsia:* 龍蝦)
Oyster (*Li huang:* 蜊蝗)
Prawn (*Ming hsia:* 明蝦)

Scallop (*Kan pei:* 干貝)
Shark's fin (*Yü chi:* 魚翅)
Shrimp (*Hsia jên:* 蝦仁)
Squid (*You yü:* 魷魚)

Fruit and Nuts
Almond (*Hsin jên:* 杏仁)
Cashew (*Yao kuo:* 腰果)
Chestnut (*Li tzǔ:* 栗子)
Date (*Tsao:* 棗)
Kumquat (*Chin chü:* 金橘)
Litchi (*Li:* 荔)
Orange (*Chü tzǔ:* 橘子)
Pear (*Li tzǔ:* 梨子)
Pineapple (*Po lo:* 菠蘿)
Strawberry (*Yang mei:* 洋莓)

Meat and Poultry
Beef (*Niu jou:* 牛肉)
Beef tongue (*Niu she:* 牛舌)
Bird's nest (*Yen won:* 燕窩)
Chicken (*Chi:* 雞)
Chicken egg (*Chi tan:* 雞蛋)
Duck (*Ya:* 鴨)
Liver (*Kan:* 肝)
Mutton (*Yang jou:* 羊肉)
Pork (*Chu jou:* 豬肉)
Quail (*An ch'un:* 鵪鶉)
Quail egg (*An ch'un tan:* 鵪鶉蛋)
Sparerib (*P'al ku:* 排骨)

Rice, Noodles and Dumplings

Congee (*Chou:* 粥)
Dumpling, meat (*Chiao tzǔ:* 餃子)
Dumpling, steamed (*Shao mai:* 燒売)
Noodles (*Mien tiao:* 麵条)
Rice, cooked (*Fan:* 飯)
Rice, glutinous (*No mi:* 糯米)
Rice, uncooked (*Ta mi:* 大米)

Seasonings and Sauces

Bean paste (*Chiang:* 醬)
Black peppercorn (*Hua chiao:* 花椒)
Chicken fat (*Chi yu:* 鶏油)
Chili pepper (*La chiao:* 辣椒)
Cornstarch-thickened sauce (*Liu:* 溜)
Garlic (*Suan:* 蒜)
Ginger (*Chiang:* 薑)
Mustard (*Chieh mo:* 芥末)
Oyster sauce (*Li huang yu:* 蜊蝗油)
Red pepper (*Hung la chiao:* 紅辣椒)
Red pepper oil (*La yu:* 辣油)
Sesame oil (*Ma yu:* 蔴油)
Sesame seeds (*Chih ma:* 芝蔴)
Soy sauce (*Chiang yu:* 醬油)
Star aniseed (*Pa chiao:* 八角)
Sweet-and-sour sauce (*T'ang ts'u:* 糖醋)
Vinegar (*Ts'u:* 醋)

Vegetables

Asparagus (*Lung hsu ts'ai:* 龍須菜)
Bamboo shoot (*Sun:* 筍)
Bean curd (*Tou fu:* 豆腐)
Bean sprout (*Tou ya ts'ai:* 豆芽菜)
Broccoli (*Chieh lan ts'ai:* 芥蘭菜)
Cabbage (*Chuan hsin ts'ai:* 捲心菜)
Cabbage, Chinese (*Pai ts'ai:* 白菜)
Carrot (*Hu lu p'o:* 胡蘿蔔)
Cauliflower (*Ts'ai hua:* 菜花)
Celery (*Ch'in ts'ai:* 芹菜)
Cucumber (*Huang kua:* 黃瓜)
Eggplant (*Ch'ieh tzǔ:* 茄子)
Green pea (*Wan tou:* 莞豆)
Green pepper (*Ch'ing chiao:* 青椒)
Leek (*Ts'ung:* 葱)
Lima bean (*Tan tou:* 蠶豆)
Lotus root (*Ou:* 藕)
Mushroom (*Tung ku:* 冬菇)
Onion (*Yang ts'ung:* 洋葱)
Pumpkin (*Nan kua:* 南瓜)
Soy bean (*Ta tou:* 大豆)
Spinach (*Po ts'ai:* 菠菜)
Sweet bean paste (*Tou sa:* 豆沙)
Sweet potato (*Pai shu:* 白薯)
Tomato (*Fan Ch'ieh:* 蕃茄)
Turnip (*Lu po:* 蘿蔔)
Vermicelli (*Fên ssu:* 粉糸)

Index